Christ's Scope and Scepter

His Word, His World

ROBERTO GAZGA

Christ's Scope and Scepter: His Word, His World

ISBN: [979-8-9917305-0-1]

Copyright © 2024 by Roberto Gazga. All rights reserved. No portion of this book may be reproduced, stored in a retrieval system, or transmitted in any form or by any means, except for brief quotations in printed reviews, without prior permission of Roberto Gazga. Requests may be submitted by email: *urbanpuritano@gmail.com*.

All Scripture quotations not otherwise designated are taken from the New King James Version®. Copyright © 1982 by Thomas Nelson. Used by permission. All rights reserved.

Scripture quotations marked "ESV" are taken from The Holy Bible, English Standard Version. ESV® Text Edition: 2016. Copyright © 2001 by Crossway Bibles, a publishing ministry of Good News Publishers.

Scripture quotations marked "NASB" are taken from the New American Standard Bible®, Copyright © 1960, 1971, 1977, 1995, 2020 by The Lockman Foundation. All rights reserved.

Scripture quotations marked "NIV" are taken from the Holy Bible, New International Version®, NIV® Copyright ©1973, 1978, 1984, 2011 by Biblica, Inc.® Used by permission. All rights reserved worldwide.

Editing services by ChristianEditingandDesign.com.

To Marta and Monica:
Calvinist, Christocentric prayer warriors

Contents

Acknowledgments	7
Foreword	9
Preface	15
Introduction	19
Part 1: The Word	24
Chapter 1: Butchers, Biblicists, or Bereans?	25
Chapter 2: Confessional Calvinists	35
Part 2: The Warrior	64
Chapter 3: Zion and David?	65
Chapter 4: Brief Excursus Concerning Zion	83
Chapter 5: Jerusalem and Jesus	89
Part 3: The World	102
Chapter 6: The Challenge of Christian Education	103
Chapter 7: The Antithesis Confirmed: Science and History	119
Chapter 8: The Antithesis Confirmed: Language and Math	127
Chapter 9: Concluding Remarks	139
Appendix	143

Acknowledgments

I want to thank all my public school teachers and coaches from kindergarten through twelfth grade for their investment in all their students, among whom I was a quietly mischievous one. Also, thanks to all my Sunday school teachers during the same time who planted the spiritual seeds that would later be watered by faithful pastors into a living faith in the Christ of Scripture.

I owe a great debt of gratitude to Pastor Brandon Myers, the Pastoral Assistants, elders, and the congregation of Christ the King Reformed Baptist Church. They stand shoulder to shoulder with members carrying out their various vocations and it was shown during the difficult pandemic response where rights were trampled on and livelihoods were at stake.

It was during the pandemic that Urban Puritano Podcast and urbanpuritano.com were born. Our message of promoting the Gospel, the whole counsel of God, and bringing Reformed theology to bear where the rubber meets the road in the life of the church and the world is simply our expression of living unto God. It would not have been possible if it were not for N. Moises Jaques of Pilgrim Digital whose creativity and expertise are limitless. Let's keep on making content in service of people in the pew and pastors behind the pulpit, brother!

Many thanks also to the staff at Christian Editing and Design for their support in finalizing the production of this small work.

Foreword

Man shall not live on bread alone, but on every word that comes from the mouth of God.

(Matthew 4:4 NIV)

"Pastor, would you please pray for me? I am struggling to read the Bible."

Over the last fourteen years of pastoral ministry in the local church, this refrain (or a sentiment very similar) is one I have heard time and time again. This has come from Christians of virtually all phases of life and every educational background (with the exception perhaps of many new believers). The State of the Church surveys put out every two years by the late R. C. Sproul's Ligonier Ministries as well as many other national surveys consistently show an uphill battle for every biblically faithful, historically orthodox Christian who seeks to contend for the faith once delivered for all the saints (Jude

1:3). The landscape of Christianity in the West in general, and the United States of America in particular, is marked by biblical illiteracy yet even worse—deliberate—that is, a chosen ignorance of the Scriptures.

This unsurprisingly has led to a decay of doctrine in the souls of many self-professing Christians and a shallowness among many if not most local churches. There is little to no confidence and assurance in the sufficiency, inerrancy, and unique unrivaled authority of the written Word of God. Why? Well, many claim, "After all, when it comes to the Bible, it's all a matter of one's interpretation, so who can be right?"

The situation is often only exacerbated when we look at the present state of theological education. Many so-called evangelical scholars training current and future evangelical pastors today care far more about being respected in the eyes of the deceived scholarly world over humbly fearing and following the living God according to the whole counsel of His Word. Pastors, then, with a diminished view of Scripture, turn to gimmicks and tricks of leadership gurus and functionally abandon the Scriptures that uniquely bear witness to Christ (John 5:39) in whom unsearchable riches are found (Ephesians 3:8).

Moreover, today many who claim to be confessional and convictional Protestants openly or secretly seem to scoff at some of the core ideas that led to the Reformation and a recovery of so much sound doctrine that was muted in favor of tradition, superstition, and mysticism. The interpretation of the written, revealed Word of God can be and often is a demanding task. But it is always worth it as the God-breathed Scriptures are the vital core of a true God-fearing Christian's discipleship. The Lord

Jesus in His high priestly prayer asked the Father, "Sanctify them in the truth; your word is truth" (John 17:17 ESV).

Yet this is why Roberto Gazga's book before you now is so needed and important, and I highly recommend it to you. Faithful local church pastors and elders (vocational or lay), Bible teachers, and Christian professors especially ought to take up this book and carefully read this (though I truly think most all Christians should as well). Roberto's book is not just another book on interpreting the Bible (hermeneutics), though it will help you wisely interpret the Bible and delight in it. Roberto's book is also not merely a polemic, though he will bless you as he rightly and precisely pushes back on some increasingly popular but incorrect paradigms in our day. Roberto's book is also not simply a blessing for the sources he probes and gem quotes he has dug up that will bless you— though it will do this as well! Rather, Roberto's book before you is an invitation and a plea for Christ's blood-bought church to live under Christ's lordship and to do so not according to our wits and whims but according to the Word of God.

Our Lord directed people to the Scriptures claiming that they spoke of and would direct people to Him (John 5:39). Even in the first century, our Lord encountered and countered religious leaders who neglected the Scriptures for the traditions of men (Mark 7:6–13). Our Lord clearly cared about and asked about the content of the law (Luke 10:25–37) and countered the devil himself with the very written words of God-breathed Scripture (Luke 4:1–13). The holy text of Scripture is for the Christian what water is for the fish and food is for the daily life of all creatures. We will starve or die spiritually without Scripture. As Brother Roberto rightly reminds us, "Interpreters, at whatever stage of maturity, have to get their hands dirty in handling the text."

It is personal to you and me and every Christian. Why? Because God does not treat His Word lightly like we so often do. In fact, the way God is glorified by His people is never around or ignoring the Word but always through and with and under the Word. God takes His Word with the utmost seriousness, and so must we. Roberto writes as a thoughtful and committed churchman seeking God's glory in all things. As you read, you will see and feast your mind on truth. Truth always has great earthly and eternal consequences, and Roberto knows this and believes it. This brother humbly presents the written, revealed Word of God and helpfully brings in faithful voices from the past who can aid us today in our present crisis, helping us grow in discernment.

Roberto's book is not only an invitation from a faithful churchman; it is also a challenge in the best sense of the word. Every single Christian from the least to the most mature must beware of and reject intellectual laziness and simply adopting Christian fads even among intellectuals (Proverbs 18:17). Whether you are a Christian who is a fresh, new convert or a seasoned pastor or tenured professor with a PhD, you and all of us must remember we have the mind of Christ (1 Corinthians 2:16); and as such, we are to discern God's will and honor God with our minds (Romans 12:2; 1 Peter 1:13; Philippians 4:8; Colossians 3:2).

Though the Lord tells us His Word never returns void (Isaiah 55), and though through their faithfulness to the Lord and His Word our forebears turned the world upside down (Acts 17:6), and though believing faith comes through hearing and hearing through the Word of Christ (Romans 10:17), many now seem to believe based on their ministries and lives "I will do everything. The Word can do nothing" (reversing Martin Luther's famous "I did nothing. The Word did everything"). Indeed, this appears to be the norm rather than the exception.

I praise God for this book and commend it to you. Read it carefully in this present evil age. Hear what is being said. Think hard about the arguments being made and truths being proposed. Do the hard work and think carefully and prayerfully with your local church family about the role of God's Word in your life and in your church. What role does the Scripture have in your life? In your family's life? In your local church's life? In the world? And if you see shortcomings or a less-than-biblical place for the Bible, what shall be done? The God of glorious grace opens the door for repentance and change of mind. Confess this sin and reorient yourself afresh under Christ's lordship. Praise be to God! As Brother Roberto reminds us in this volume, "We have, in the text of Scripture from beginning to end, God's strategic wisdom and tactical cunning summed up in the person and work of Christ."

May this book be used by the Lord to help individual Christians and many local churches recover or renew their desire and commitment to have the mind of Christ. May the glory of God's Word in the verses below bearing witness to God's grace and truth in Christ the Redeemer become an increasing reality in every reader's life, as well as every family, every local church, every community, and every school:

The Law of Your mouth is better to me Than thousands of gold and silver pieces. (Psalm 119:72)

The words of the Lord are pure words; As silver tried in a furnace on the earth, refined seven times. (Psalm 12:6)

The precepts of the LORD are right, rejoicing the heart; The commandment of the LORD is pure, enlightening the eyes. (Psalm 19:8)

But know this first of all, that no prophecy of Scripture is a matter of one's own interpretation, for no prophecy was ever made by an act of human will, but men moved by the Holy Spirit spoke from God. (2 Peter 1:20–21)

And He said to them, "O foolish men and slow of heart to believe in all that the prophets have spoken! Was it not necessary for the Christ to suffer these things and to enter into His glory?" Then beginning with Moses and with all the prophets, He explained to them the things concerning Himself in all the Scriptures. (Luke 24:25–27)

Soli Deo Gloria

Brandon Myers
Senior Pastor of Christ the King Reformed Baptist Church, Niles IL
May 2024

Preface

What does the Lord Jesus have to do with interpreting both God's Word and God's world?

Conventional wisdom puts the cart before the horse, claiming that the world, whether scholarship or popular opinion, must dictate how the Bible is to be interpreted and who Jesus really is. Most critical scholarship argues that the world is a self-contained, self-explanatory system. It asserts that the Bible contains no overarching metanarrative and should be relegated to a haphazard arrangement of tales. It argues that Jesus was an itinerant rabbi who died a martyr's death and later became the founding figure of a community of followers. In doing so, conventional wisdom gets the world, the Word, and the Lord Jesus woefully wrong.

Christian wisdom in general and Calvinist wisdom in particular, however, self-consciously mediate and subjugate knowledge of the world according to the Jesus of the Word. In doing so, they get God's world, God's Word, and Jesus right, holding that the world is the theater of God's glory in Christ, who is the *telos* (goal) of all creation precisely because He is the *raison d'être* (fundamental reason and purpose of its existence). As the Bible says, He is the "Lamb slain from the foundation of the world" (Revelation 13:8). Calvinists observe that according to the Bible, Christ is the all-encompassing Alpha and Omega for both creation and redemption.

This Calvinist self-conscious mediation and subjugation of knowledge of the world to the Jesus of the Word is a lifelong process. It is both a science and an art. It is a science insofar as it seeks to discover further truths from the axiom of God's Word. It is an art insofar as this lifelong process can be as messy as a painter's palette.

Therefore, my present work of "art" starts within the "scientific" framework of the primacy of the Lord Jesus as revealed in God's Word. Only He, through His Word correctly understood, can get the things of this world right.

I begin and end by asking myself two questions, respectively:

- Am I a Christocentric reader?
- Am I a Christocentric teacher?

In painting, artists sometimes apply neutral colors (called *grisaille* or *bistre*) to a blank canvas as underpainting to give the work more depth and realism. In the same way, I invite the reader to look over my shoulder as I have sought to paint a portrait of Christocentrism for God's Word and God's world. Perhaps my efforts will inspire you to paint your own Christocentric work of art.

Each stroke is infused with a line of thought. What may be vibrantly seen in the final work belies the necessary tonal underpainting and the further grayscale on the canvas of my experience.

As a Calvinist Christian, I believe it is only natural and right to mediate and subjugate all of life to the primacy of the Lord Jesus as revealed in the Scriptures. He tells me He is the way, the truth, and the life. Therefore, I can see and live my knowledge of my experiences in the world only in light of Him. In His light I see light. Christians ought to take this as a joyful invitation to take the Bible seriously and "sanctify Christ as Lord in your hearts, always being ready to make a defense to everyone who asks you to give an account for the hope that is in you, but with gentleness and respect" (1 Peter 3:15 NASB).

So how have my life's experiences been shaped by the primacy and centrality of the Lord Jesus in both the Word and the world? By the grace of God I have been privileged to be called to teach children and adults in diverse settings, in both Christian elementary schools and the local churches I have been a member of. In those teaching capacities I have sought to open the Scriptures, to explain and teach God's Word to God's people.

My hope is that parents, pastors, teachers, students, and lay leaders would ponder the eternal significance of God's Word for God's world, whatever their present understanding of both are. As for me, I humbly stand upon the unbreakable rock of Reformed Christocentrism. I can do no other, so help me God.

Introduction

The Christ of Scripture is central to the believer's life. Too many Christians lack a robust understanding of this idea. It is not sufficiently fleshed out regarding hermeneutics (the branch of knowledge concerning interpretation of texts, especially Scripture), much less its applicability for the world we live in. Whether we call it Christocentric Calvinism or Reformed Christocentrism, we can gain a clearer and greater appreciation of this idea once it is incarnated in real-life reading of the Word and real-life application of that Word in the world. It is well past time for the rays of Christocentrism to escape the confines of the academy and be reflected and diffused in the church, in homes, and in the street.

This work isn't meant to be a formal theological or philosophical treatise. However, it may be more theological and philosophical than some may like. Indeed, I want to ground sound interpretation of the Word and the world upon a Christocentric foundation. But overall, my case is more impressionistic and suggestive rather than theologically and philosophically rigorous. Like Aunt Polly's prayer (from *The Adventures of Tom Sawyer* by Mark Twain), this work is "built from the ground up of solid courses of Scriptural quotations, welded together with a thin mortar of originality." For this I make no apologies.

After all, this work is deeply personal, born of reflection I was engaged in while living my calling and carrying out its duties as a teacher in the midst of an increasingly decaying and crumbling society and culture. I taught subject matter to children and adults, including an elementary school curriculum as well as the Bible respectively. Why? Because despite the cultural rot, God always has the first and last word on all matters.

Although I'm no more than an armchair Christian philosopher or theologian, I still self-consciously tried to apply analytic philosopher Alvin Plantinga's advice to Christian philosophers in his famous essay "Advice to Christian Philosophers," from 1984. He argued, "Christian philosophers must display more integrity——integrity in the sense of integral wholeness, or oneness, or unity, being all of one piece. Perhaps 'integrality' would be the better word here."[1] For our purposes, such integrality involves seeing Christ in all of Scripture for all of life.

I have two hopes, dear reader: (1) that you can adapt and integrate my work with your own experiences and (2) that

---

1 Alvin Plantinga, "Advice to Christian Philosophers," *Faith and Philosophy* 1, no. 3 (1984): 254.

you can encourage those in your sphere of influence, whether in your household, your local church, your college, or your seminary, to strive to see all of Christ in all of Scripture for all of life. Whether or not you identify with the Reformed tradition as I do, our shared faith commits all believers to seek the Lord Jesus "in whom are hidden all the treasures of wisdom and knowledge" (Colossians 2:3 NASB).

To that end, my portrait of Christocentrism according to confessional Calvinism is divided into three interdependent parts.

Part 1 will lay a foundation for biblical interpretation according to confessional Calvinism, wherein I discuss some axiomatic principles of biblical hermeneutics (that is, proper interpretation) necessary to read Scripture correctly. Historic Protestant confessions such as the Westminster Confession of Faith (WCF) or the Second London Baptist Confession of Faith (2LBCF) explicitly demand and endorse such principles.

Part 2 will provide an example of these interpretive principles applied to a challenging Old Testament text. It constitutes an extended reading for teaching and preaching Christ in the manner of passages about the roads to Emmaus (Luke 24) and Gaza (Acts 8). This will necessarily involve getting our hands dirty, for only in such a way can we rightly divide the Word of truth. We will have to employ various tools in order to judiciously and rationally draw out the text's single *sensus plenior* (fuller sense). That is, human authors in the Old Testament intended to convey a message to their audiences. God often had a concurrent redemptive-historical intention related to Jesus's ministry to convey to a future audience via the divinely inspired sacred text. After all, the recipients of Christ's Word are the people of God in all ages. He was able to do this because He alone is sovereign over both history and the process of recording the redemptive-historical events themselves. We will therefore use a robustly Reformed grammatico-historical method wedded to a Christocentric redemptive-historical approach. We will scratch the surface in addressing the right reading of figurative language and typology, simultaneously rejecting the medieval interpretive paradigm known as the *quadriga*, a word that comes from the Latin name for a chariot drawn by four horses abreast, which later became the name of an approach to hermeneutics. Various church fathers and medieval theologians up to the great Thomas Aquinas recognized four distinct meanings in Holy Writ: literal, allegorical, tropological, and anagogical. We will touch on these concepts later. Suffice it to say now that those horses don't haul.

Finally, in part 3 we will commend the fortunes of a Reformed Christian worldview as applied to some key areas of education. There is a continuity between a right reading of the Word and a right vision for the world, which the content of education inevitably deals with. No matter what model or system of education you participate in, the primacy and supremacy of the Lord Jesus is central and paramount. Whether it's a traditional Christian day school, a classical Christian school, a co-op, a homeschool, or the kitchen table for tutoring your or someone else's children entrusted to you, authentic Christian education presents a challenge worth considering by all involved. It is a challenge worth wrestling with as much as Jacob wrestled with the angel of the Lord until he received his blessing.

And so I have organized this work to commend a Reformed framework for reading the Word of Jesus to exemplify the warrior Jesus and to elucidate key issues in interpreting the world of Jesus. I encourage you to see all of Christ in all of Scripture for all of life!

PART 1:
THE WORD

*My heart is overflowing with a good theme;
I recite my composition concerning the King;
My tongue is the pen of a ready writer.*
(Psalm 45:1)

Chapter 1:
Butchers, Biblicists, or Bereans?

So Philip ran to him, and heard him reading the prophet Isaiah, and said, "Do you understand what you are reading?" And he said, "How can I, unless someone guides me?"

(Ethiopian's encounter with Philip, Acts 8:30–31)

Confessional Calvinism approaches Holy Scripture as the absolute Word of the absolute God. The Scriptures are the Word of truth from the God of truth (Deuteronomy 32:4; John 14:6; John 16:13—a Trinitarian emphasis on God as truth). This absolute confidence in the unique nature, message, and character of God's Word is inseparable from our absolute confidence in the unique nature and character of the God of truth Himself (see Psalm 138:2).

Concerning its uniqueness and its message, Reformed apologist Cornelius Van Til stated, "Nowhere but in Scripture does an absolute God speak. Nowhere but in Scripture is redemption by pure grace alone. Nowhere but in Scripture is there a program of the destruction of all sin [and] evil. Nowhere but in Scripture is there the picture of absolute victory at last."[2]

What, then, is the correct path for us to rightly interpret the vast and sweeping content of the Holy Scripture? Some appeal to extra-biblical considerations first to find orientation. They may even forget about the actual content of Scripture itself and become enamored with the deliverances of interpretive traditions about the Bible throughout Church history. Instead of "Thus saith the Lord," they prioritize "Thus saith the church." However, what makes church history any more understandable or authoritative than the Scriptures themselves? You see, not only can individuals miss the mark on correctly interpreting Scripture, but churches and a church's interpretive tradition can also miss the mark. Nevertheless, that does not leave us in a position of hopelessness or unyielding despair when it comes to a right understanding of Scripture. Primacy of place must be given to the Scriptures alone, not only over our feelings and preferences but also to whatever long-held interpretive traditions may compete, undermine, or contradict the deliverances of Scripture.

---

[2] Cornelius Van Til, foreword to *Study Your Bible: A Self Study Course for Bible Believing Christians*, by Edward J. Young (Grand Rapids, MI: Eerdmans, 1934), 3.

On Butchering or Not Butchering Scripture

We are bound to make mistakes in our interpretations of God's Word from time to time and in certain portions of Scripture or others. However, the Bible is of such a nature that if any contemporary believer arrives at a correct interpretation of a text's meaning, especially regarding God and salvation, the church in generations past surely knew and believed it.

When an interpretation of the Bible's teaching is accepted by a group of people over a period of time, whether correct or not, it's called *tradition*. The concept of tradition points us back to our primary and ultimately vital concern: the right reading or interpretation of Scripture. Why? Because the people of God must attend to His voice in Scripture. His voice is found nowhere else. The echoes of tradition are derivatively authoritative only insofar as they read and interpret Scripture right. So all believers (past, present, and future) must not put the traditional cart before the scriptural horse.

Some may scoff at this as not being epistemologically self-aware. After all, we all come with ideas, presuppositions, and biases. Indeed we do. However, since mistakes are inevitable, we must choose to "sin boldly" in posturing ourselves before God's Word first and foremost since this element of "method" is what is held forth in Scripture itself: "Today, if you hear His voice" (Hebrews 1–3 as a reminder).

Moreover, a question that both our Lord Jesus and His apostles never tired of asking (Matthew 21:42; Romans 4:3) is "Have you never read in the Scriptures?" or "What does the Scripture say?" In reality, this Holy Spirit-inspired question revealed and recorded in the Scriptures is the one from the voice of God to which all other questions, even venerated tradition, must bow. The voice of Scripture is the voice of God. Scripture alone is God's supremely primary speech to the world.

Everyone, including believers, possesses control beliefs and assumed schema that the course of our lives will either confirm or disconfirm. Instead of rightly dividing the Word of truth, we are always in danger of wrongly dividing—butchering—it. It is not only the simple believer who will have to learn and unlearn certain baggage of previously held beliefs. Academics and scholars will too—perhaps more so! Instead of butchering the Word, we as careful Christians will be butchering and mortifying our own false notions about Scripture through Scripture as time goes on. Our growth in reading and interpreting Scripture correctly will be guided by the avoidance of twin errors: being mistaken from not knowing the Scriptures (Matthew 22:29) and being mistaken from not knowing the power of God (Mark 12:24). The knowledge of Scripture and the power of God through Scripture are present realities not cut off from any of God's people. We are and always have been a people of the Word.

Faith comes to us by hearing and hearing by the word of God (Romans 10:17). So then, we are concerned with getting our hands dirty and handling the Bible in order to read and interpret it correctly. The Scripture describes right reading and interpretation as "rightly dividing the word of truth" (2 Timothy 2:15). How do we proceed?

First, let us define what we mean by "interpretation." *Second,* we must answer why "interpretation" is even necessary. *Third,* we will suggest a basic roadmap, as it were, for interpreting the Scriptures for ourselves.

What Is Interpretation?

Interpretation refers to the opening up, the explanation, of the words and statements of Scripture in order to draw out their single, full, and natural meaning (Westminster Confession of Faith, chapter 1, sections 7 and 9). This confessional Calvinism necessarily excludes all arbitrary and capricious medieval or quadriga-like conceptions of the interpretive task. Church history tells us that Scripture sets forth four interpretations. The literal is the plain meaning of the text, especially where it relates to what happened. It becomes a springboard to find three other encompassing spiritual meanings: allegorical (what to believe), tropological (how to act), and anagogical (hope of heaven). Figurative or spiritual interpretations often take the form of fanciful allegories that do not so much explain the meaning of the text as they obscure it with the interpreter's cleverness.

In contrast, true interpretation involves—

1. negatively, removing differences and distance between the original authors and readers today; and
2. positively, providing a firm hermeneutical foundation and appropriate exegetical tools to build a solid framework for the inevitable construction of a coherent theology. For every interpretation and meaning arrived at, there must be a justifiable rationale for it. Furthermore, there is no dualistic bifurcation between the literal and the spiritual meaning of Scripture.

Hermeneutics, the science of interpreting Scripture, is not meant to be daunting. Exegesis, the art of drawing out the meaning from Scripture, is not meant to be intimidating.

Indeed, average persons can confirm for themselves by surveying and reading Scripture that it is generally clear in its message from cover to cover, especially regarding God and salvation. Are there some portions of Scripture that are more difficult to understand than others? Yes. Does this justify the lazy and erroneous conclusion that the Bible says whatever the interpreter wants it to say? No.

There is, after all, such a thing as a correct mental grasp of meaning on the one hand and an incorrect mental grasp of meaning on the other hand.[3] To apprehend Scripture's correct meaning is to understand. Failing to apprehend the Scripture's correct meaning is to misunderstand. The former leads to a knowledge of the truth. The latter does not.

When it comes to meaning, then, Scripture is not schizophrenic, neither in whole nor in part.

Why Is Interpretation Even Necessary?

We the interpreters of Scripture are indeed spiritually schizophrenic. We hear and obey the conflicting voices of our own imaginations, traditions, cultures, education, morals, customs, tastes, loyalties, preferences, aversions, and affections (or those of other people). Not all voices are equal. Even the voice of tradition, however great it may be, must be weighed in the biblical balance. These many voices bid us to go down different paths of interpretation.

Remember, though, that the Scriptures are not an unintelligible cacophony but a symphonic communication.

---

[3] Robert H. Stein, *A Basic Guide to Interpreting the Bible: Playing by the Rules*, 2nd ed. (Grand Rapids, MI: Baker Academic, 2011), 44.

Apart from the foundational recognition that the Scriptures are divinely designed revelation and as such are rationally intelligible, the paths of interpretation are as inconsistent as they are uncertain. Indeed, apart from this foundational recognition, is not despair in the interpretive task warranted?

Being a Christian does not in and of itself safeguard the interpreter from error. Simply being a Christian and recognizing Scripture's divine character is no guarantee of interpretive success. Christians didn't just fall from heaven as impartial, objective angels with a correct conception of scriptural revelation. Who among us is not born into unique historical and cultural milieus? We all very naturally rely on our own intellectual, emotional, moral, educational, traditional, historical, and spiritual resources to guide us in our interpretative tasks. Humility acknowledges that although our spirits are willing to be good interpreters of Scripture, our flesh is weak.

Parallel to this situation, we must recognize that even the Bible itself did not descend from on high to each and every one of us in our own language, cultural patterns, or period of history. Although we must not exaggerate the "hermeneutic distance" to render our interpretive task hopeless, we must not minimize it either. The life and times of the biblical writers and their accounts are different than our own. And even if we lived in biblical times and places, there would still exist difficulties of interpreting God's Word.

Difficulties, not impossibilities.

The ground of the interpreters' hope is that Scripture is a communication from God! Interpretive despair, therefore, is unwarranted. Thankfully, we can also draw comfort in Peter's declaration that some things in Paul's writings "are hard to understand, which the ignorant and unstable twist to their own destruction, as they do the other Scriptures" (2 Peter 3:16 ESV).

These obstacles to interpretation, therefore, highlight the necessity for interpretation. Obstacles exist both within us and outside of us—within us due to a myriad of limitations exacerbated by sin, outside of us due to the distance of time, history, culture, and the difference between language and thought patterns between the Scriptures and ourselves.

I want to commend a confessionally Calvinistic, indeed, a thoroughly Reformed approach to biblical interpretation that can be built upon for personal use, an approach that takes seriously the variety of terrain the biblical landscape displays in all its diversity of stylistic traits and its rich, abstract theological features. My hope is that this Reformed approach to biblical interpretation can begin to yield God-glorifying results along the lines of both (1) a panoramic Christ-ward and Christ-centered (John 5:39, 45–47) view of God's redemptive, overarching story and message for man; and (2) a symphonic (not schizophrenic), spiritual hearing of God's redemptive composition called sacred Scripture. As Revelation 3:22 tells us, "Whoever has ears, let them hear what the Spirit says" (NIV).

As we begin our journey, let us keep ever present the fact that a truly efficacious and spiritual understanding of God's Word never precludes that it can be submitted to the categories of logical analysis and scrutiny. The Bible won't wither away under our investigations. In fact, God invites, welcomes, and commends honest investigation and interpretation (Acts 17:11)—involving neither butchers nor an ill-defined strawman term like *biblicist,* which I explore in detail in the appendix. What then? So help us through the triune God of Scripture—we can be Bereans!

CHAPTER 2:
Confessional Calvinists

"Good Morning!" said Bilbo, and he meant it. . . .
"What do you mean?" he said. "Do you wish me a good morning, or mean that it is a good morning whether I want it or not; or that you feel good this morning; or that it is a morning to be good on?"
"All of them at once," said Bilbo.[4]

(Bilbo's encounter with Gandalf, the premodern scholastic, and his pre-critical quadriga)

Confessional Calvinists are many things. However, as they grow in conscientiousness and intentionality concerning their reading of Scripture, they certainly strive to eschew butchering the text. They also strive to eschew ill-defined biblicism. Perhaps biblicism is a naive view or approach to

---
4   J. R. R. Tolkien, *The Hobbit* (Boston: Houghton Mifflin, 1966), 17–18.

Scripture that seeks to explain Scripture without the help of external categories or resources. I don't know. Some ill-define it one way while others ill-define it another way. Biblicism has evolved into a popular pejorative term among academically oriented interpreters of the Bible and their all-too-eager seminarian whippersnapper acolytes. But as I stated in the last section above, a believer's understanding of the interpretive task grows. Thankfully, the third option is a biblical one: Berean believers (Acts 17:10–15)!

The Berean believers attended the voice of God in Scripture and confirmed the validity of the apostle Paul's conclusions by means of Scripture. In doing so, they merited the commendation of being noble or fair-minded in searching the Scriptures daily to find out if the things Paul preached and taught were so. There was no need for confessional pearl-clutching. We can do the same as the Bereans did since we all have the same starting place—the Bible.

The Bible is an extraordinarily normal, worldly book. Its familiarity and similarity to other world literature is undeniable. At the same time, however, it is an extraordinarily unique and supernatural book. Despite having been written by over forty authors over a fifteen-hundred-year period, covering historical events in methodical, logical progression from diverse cultural viewpoints, the Scriptures consistently tell us about God and ourselves. Cornelius Van Til correctly observed that for the faithful reader, "Sacred history becomes terrible and beautiful. It grips one in the inmost depths of his existence. There is no epic so sweeping, no drama so dramatic as the story of sacred history when told after the Reformed conception of it."[5]

The Bible is also an otherworldly revelation. Its transcendent character and content are undeniable as well. Sacred Scripture reveals the God of whom it speaks and His Word's universal applicability to man's existence by revealing his true nature and plight. Throughout its diverse pages, its unity in message is sufficiently perceived, resulting in either humble embrace or judgmental rejection. The Bible reads the reader and demands response!

This revelation will not be content merely as one among many. It unravels the reader while the reader wrestles with and attempts to unravel it—"terrible and beautiful" indeed. It is "terrible" in the sense of the weightiness of the subject matter. The Scriptures deal with no light matters. What or who is the God of whom it speaks? What or who is the humanity to whom it speaks? How can an utterly just and holy God commune with utterly sinful and rebellious people? Trembling is the appropriate response.

It is beautiful in the sense of the *comfort* His Word proffers, which details God's gracious intention to ultimately display His refulgent radiance in His redemptive work and communion with His people. This is love in its ultimate possible expression: not our love toward God but the other way around. Omnipotent, immeasurable, undeserving love toward us made our salvation both possible and actual. In His Word, we find the only comfort in life and death, symmetry,

---

[5] Cornelius Van Til, foreword to *Study Your Bible: A Self Study Course for Bible Believing Christians*, by Edward J. Young (Grand Rapids, MI: Eerdmans, 1934), 3–4.

vibrancy, every brush stroke, all the pieces to the puzzle, all the threads on the tapestry, every note in the musical score, and every square inch of creation, providence, and redemption redound to His glory and graciously to our good. This is nothing less than the posture of confessional Calvinism.

Where can the interpreter begin? No doubt, all interpreters begin somewhere, and although there is an "interplay between broader principles of interpretation and particular texts,"[6] it would be fruitful to briefly delineate some of those assumed hermeneutical principles that underlie our interpretation of particular texts.

Thus, the following underlying, general hermeneutical assumptions are a good place to start before we concentrate our focus further. I have already alluded to some of them. Now I will expand upon all of them throughout the rest of this chapter as interlocking links in a chain:

1. The verbal and plenary inspiration of Scripture
2. The perspicuity of Scripture
3. The analogy of Scripture and the analogy of faith
4. The unity and diversity of Scripture

1. THE VERBAL AND PLENARY INSPIRATION OF SCRIPTURE
The verbal and plenary inspiration of Scripture refers to the Scriptures being the product of God causing the various biblical authors to write down everything exactly as He intended. This includes not only the big ideas or major portions of Scripture; this divine causation extends to the

---

6 Vern S. Poythress, "Biblical Hermeneutics," in *Seeing Christ in All of Scripture: Hermeneutics at Westminster Theological Seminary*, ed. Peter A. Lillback (Philadelphia: Westminster Seminary Press, 2016), 9.

whole, inclusive of every word itself. Furthermore, this divine inspiration was neither mechanical nor in any way subversive of human authorship whatsoever. Whatever human effort was involved in the prewriting process and whatever style the authors employed in the writing process itself, God ensured by this divine inspiration that His thoughts and the writers' thoughts interpenetrated such that various authors recorded a bona fide communication from God to His people exactly as He intended.

The presupposition of the verbal and plenary inspiration of Scripture, like all the other underlying hermeneutical assumptions we will adduce, is not postulated simply by theological imposition. It emerges quite naturally from passages such as 2 Timothy 3:16; 2 Peter 1:19–21; and 1 Corinthians 2:7–13, among many other texts throughout Scripture. For further study, see Louis Gaussen's *Theopneustia*, B. B. Warfield's *Inspiration and Authority of the Bible,* and Greg Beale's more recent *Erosion of Inerrancy.*

Before moving on, I would be remiss in my Reformed duty if I failed to point out that this classical evangelical view of the verbal and plenary inspiration of Scripture is actually a major illustration and example of the Calvinistic understanding of concurrence between the will of God and the will of man. If divine causation results in man willfully writing down exactly what God intends (e.g., the writing of Scripture), is there any other area in which divine causation results in man willing something or other precisely as God intends? (Calvinists, mischievously or not, answer yes).

Let the careless reader beware if he comes to the biblical text presupposing by default the concept of libertarian free will, the principle of alternative possibilities (especially for genuine love to exist), or the pop-Arminian notion that God is a "gentleman" who must always respect autonomous human choice in order to be able to hold us responsible for our actions. Sooner rather than later, the reader will collide with texts that are incompatible with such deeply erroneous notions. Neither the biblical authors nor much less the biblical God conforms to the false assumptions bound up with libertarian free will.

2. The Perspicuity of Scripture

The perspicuity of Scripture refers to the basic quality of clarity the Scriptures exhibit as a whole, but especially in regard to the question "What must I do to be saved?" The Westminster Confession of Faith is most excellent in this regard. Chapter 1, section 7, states, "All things in Scripture are not alike plain in themselves, nor alike clear unto all, yet those things which are necessary to be known, believed and observed, for salvation, are so clearly propounded and opened in some place of Scripture or other, that not only the learned, but the unlearned, in due use of the ordinary means, may attain unto a sufficient understanding of them."

By What Means?

As Reformed teacher R. C. Sproul aptly put it, "Biblical Christianity is not an esoteric religion."[7] The means of biblical interpretation do not involve mysterious practices yielding

---

[7] R. C. Sproul, *Knowing Scripture* (Downers Grove: InterVarsity Press, 1977), 16.

mysterious meanings. There is no meaning in Scripture other than what the "due use of the ordinary means" will yield. Therefore, our fundamental concern is to remain so close to the text that only what is "expressly" (explicitly) written in Scripture or what "by good and necessary consequence may be deduced" from Scripture is privileged (WCF, chapter 1, section 6).

This interpretive guardrail is both rational and biblical. It is *Berean*! Remember: biblical interpretation means attending to the voice of God present in Scripture. The burden of the believer is to rightly understand the words of Scripture, the communicative intent of both the divine and human authors, and what can rightly follow from what is expressed and how it is expressed. A wonderful example of this Berean approach on display in a theological debate on a biblical topic was when Dr. Joseph Pipa masterfully gave a reasoned defense for limited atonement and successfully attacked Dave Hunt's unlimited atonement view.[8] Dr. Pipa did not clutch his confessional pearls, but he adduced Scripture and rightly divided the Word of Truth to be persuasive so that the confidence of everyone present could be in *sola scriptura*. To adduce Scripture and give the meaning through analysis and synthesis is not a naive stacking of verses. Who would be so arrogant or disingenuous as to ascribe *solo* or *nuda scriptura* to an Apollos-like defense of biblical doctrine given by Dr. Pipa or any simple believer for that matter?

The perspicuity of Scripture recognizes that some portions or texts of Scripture may not easily yield their meaning and

---

8   "Calvinism Debate Joseph Pipa vs Dave Hunt," November 27, 2021, video, https://www.youtube.com/watch?v=LbdD40rGVFs.

may be difficult to understand. As mentioned earlier, the apostle Peter said as much concerning some of the apostle Paul's writings that are among portions of Scripture (2 Peter 3:15–16). But the solution to a charley horse between the ears is, as Reformed philosopher and theologian Gordon Clark would say, "a rational massage." The perspicuity of Scripture thus does not demand that the meaning of Scripture "always lie[s] on the surface."[9] There is, after all, the legitimacy, if not the inevitability and indispensability, of logical implications in communication that the Scriptures themselves are not exempt from. What believer would argue against God's Word having logical depth?

This logical depth, however, is not something beyond the words of Scripture rightly understood. This is key. "Beyond" the words of Scripture cannot mean distinct or separate from the communicative intent revealed by the words themselves and their relationship with other words and portions of Scripture. No text of Scripture is an island unto itself. This is ultimately because of divine design.

Interpretations must always have a rational rationale. The whole enterprise of biblical hermeneutics and exegesis is essentially a rational method applied to a rational revelation. Together, they are an artful science seeking to rationally and judiciously arrive at the correct meaning of the biblical text. Its foundations, principles, and methods are thoroughly rational and coherent within themselves and with Scripture.

---

[9] Louis Berkhof, *Principles of Biblical Interpretation* (Grand Rapids, MI: Baker Book House, 1950), 59.

By Whom?

Gordon Clark correctly notes, "The Bible has a message intended to be understood." By whom? By a select group of elite academicians, scholars, gurus, or clerics? By only a special class of people who alone are tasked with its interpretation and who are to dole out its meaning to the masses? In standard Protestant form, Clark matter-of-factly states the Reformation's dangerous idea: "The Bible was addressed to the populace at large—the working men and slaves as well as to kings and those in authority."

That God intends ordinary people to understand the Bible does not preclude other individuals, the academy, or a community of faith from being of help to a person struggling with the correct interpretation of a biblical text. It does not preclude interpretive tradition from being of help either. Tradition can be a friend. Remember: the Bible is of such a nature that if any believer nowadays arrives at a correct interpretation of a text's meaning, especially regarding God and salvation, the church has surely known and believed it in the past. God's Word is perspicuous to God's people. The perspicuity of Scripture simply recognizes that correct interpretation is within everyone's reach and is not dependent on a special class of official interpreters or only those who tap into tradition.

Very pointedly Clark drives the point home: "If you and I are so stupid as not to be able to understand the Bible, but need priests, bishops, and popes [or tradition, however great it may be] to tell us what it means, are we not also too stupid to understand what [they] say?"[10]

---

10   Gordon H. Clark, *What Do Presbyterians Believe?* (Phillipsburg: P&R Publishing, 1965), 23.

Thankfully, and by grace alone, the Scripture's content and overarching storyline composed of myriad "stories, examples, precepts, exhortations, admonitions, and promises"[11] concerning God's redemptive purpose and man's salvation are sufficiently "clear and evident." Both scholar and layman can by the same means arrive at the answer to how a holy and just God can bless rebellious, sinful mankind with salvation. As it was before for shepherds, warriors, royalty, and fishermen and as it continued to be for monks, maidens, lawyers, and tinkers, so the Bible's message continues now—sufficiently "clear and evident" to all who would apply "a due use of the ordinary means."

3. THE ANALOGY OF SCRIPTURE AND THE ANALOGY OF FAITH

Given the nature of the Bible alone as the Word of God, given that the voice of God is found in Scripture alone, how might a believer be rightly attuned to listening to what God has spoken? Given the verbal and plenary inspiration of Holy Scripture through human and divine dimensions that resulted in an overarchingly clear message for God's people throughout all of time, what other foundational principles did they have a bearing on? In consonance with and in consequence of the hermeneutical assumptions mentioned previously (i.e., the verbal and plenary inspiration of the Scripture and the perspicuity of Scripture), the confessional Calvinist can further adduce the two-pronged principle or dual principles: the analogy of Scripture and the analogy

---

[11] William Ames, *The Marrow of Theology* (Grand Rapids, MI: Baker Books, 1997), 187–88.

of faith. These principles refer to "the uniform teaching of Scripture" (analogy of faith) by means of Scripture itself (analogy of Scripture).[12]

In other words, Scripture interpreting Scripture (analogy of Scripture) inevitably leads to a clear, uniform teaching and theology from Scripture as a whole (analogy of faith). These principles are consummately functional and practical, and once distinguished properly and not conflated, they will be lifelong companions to the Berean interpreter to safeguard against butchering the text from taking place. If the text of Scripture has in fact been butchered by someone or by a tradition, Scripture can correct the error.

The WCF chapter 1, section 9, states, "The infallible rule of Scripture is Scripture itself; and therefore, when there is a question about the true and full sense of any Scripture (which is not manifold, but one), it must be *searched and known* by other places that speak more clearly" (emphasis added). Why? Because s*ola scriptura* and *tota scriptura* are the only "rule of faith and life" for the confessional Calvinist (WCF chapter 1, section 2; same with the 2LBCF). This is truly a workman's hermeneutic. The analogy of Scripture impels us to do the hard work of searching the Scriptures, as the Bereans did, while the analogy of faith safeguards the deposit of sound doctrine to be known.

Note that in describing the analogy of Scripture, the WCF also affirms and denies certain things about the meaning or sense of Scripture. To the respective questions about whether any particular Bible passage has multiple meanings

---

12 Berkhof, *Principles*, 26.

and whether any particular Scripture passage has only one meaning, the answers given by the confession are:
- No, the true sense of Scripture is not manifold of which is necessarily included the pre-critical quadriga (and by implication even post-modern multiplicity of meanings).
- Yes, the true and full sense of any Scripture is one.

The sense or meaning of Scripture can be enhanced in such a way that one can arrive at a fuller comprehension of the text under consideration with the help of other texts of Scripture. This fuller understanding has recently been ambiguously described by some wanting to integrate the pre-critical quadriga into Protestant hermeneutics as levels of meaning. But this erroneous pre-modern conception of hermeneutics attempting to make a contemporary comeback in Protestant academia, conceived the deeper levels of scriptural meaning as distinct double, triple, or quadruple meanings, whereas the WCF and 2LBCF rightly and explicitly limit the sense or meaning of Scripture to being singular or one.

THE PRE-MODERN QUADRIGA: A BUTCHER?

The Quadriga is a medieval Roman Catholic academic method of interpreting the Bible that bifurcates the literal sense of Scripture from its spiritual sense. The literal sense consists of whatever meaning the words of Scripture render in ordinary ways derivable from a consideration of linguistics, philology, semantics, grammar, syntax, and historical considerations of its content. The spiritual sense of Scripture consists of 3 further distinct domains of meaning yielding:

- Allegory or figurative signs used to signify something else
- Tropology or moral lessons and imperatives
- Anagogy or future focused eschatological hope

These three senses encompass the spiritual significance of Scripture statements in contrast and contra-distinction to the literal sense of Scripture.

Some pastors, theologians, and seminaries may commend the division of the sense of Scripture into four senses: the literal (grammatical-historico), the allegorical (symbolic/spiritual), the tropological (moral), and the anagogical (future/eschatological) senses of Scriptural meaning. This quadriga is gaining respect in some quarters. An academic yet erroneous way of explaining away the confession's denial of manifold meaning by some Protestants is to quickly affirm that the extra-literal meaning is spiritual and that it is never divorced from the literal sense. But despite its traditional pedigree, such an arbitrary and capricious dissection is both anti-confessional and unbiblical. It is, therefore, most unworthy of retrieval in either thick or thin forms.

The Reformed denial of the manifold sense of Scripture is irreconcilable with the Quadriga's fourfold sense or even its attempted re-imagining two-fold bifurcation of the literal and spiritual senses of Scripture. Interestingly, neither past stalwarts, contemporary academics, nor their seminarian whippersnapper acolytes have ever argued that the literal meaning should be based on the allegorical, tropological, or anagogical meanings. The literal sense has priority even when the quadriga is held as a legitimate method of biblical interpretation.

The priority of the literal sense, however, hints at an argument for the Calvinist's confessional single-sense theory of scriptural meaning. To wit: All true meaning of Scripture is derived from the literal sense. Any allegorical, symbolic, figural, typological, moral, or eschatological meaning of Scripture, if genuinely true, is derivative of the literal sense. Therefore, two things follow: (1) the sense of Scripture is not manifold, but one; and (2) the literal sense and no other constitutes the singular and genuinely true sense of Scripture. (See William Whitaker's book *Disputations on Holy Scripture* for more on this and many other arguments that found confessional status in the WCF.) Despite its attempted rehabilitation in academia, the quadriga should find little appeal to serious readers of Scripture, especially by those who claim to be Evangelicals or confessional Calvinists.

Should the believer's sensibilities and interpretive virtues be guided by respect for this premodern fourfold sense grid? No. If Biblical interpretation must yield a fourfold sense of Scripture, why four? This is arbitrary. If Biblical interpretation must not always yield a fourfold sense of Scripture, why not? This is capricious. To do interpretation by quadriga, then, is not exegesis but eisegesis. No method of biblical hermeneutics that is either capricious or arbitrary is biblically legitimate. The quadriga is disqualified as being a legitimate hermeneutical tool by being both capricious and arbitrary.

The confessional Calvinist, on the other hand, by adherence to a single-sense theory of Scripture can arrive at the single *sensus plenior* by a myriad of non-arbitrary and non-capricious methods. The inductive analysis of Scripture afforded by the analogy of Scripture takes into account the text's diverse features without bifurcating the literal from the spiritual, the Old Testament from the New Testament, or a single passage from its canon-wide context. For this reason, most talk cautioning against atomistic reading of Scripture is misguided. At least for the confessional Calvinist since there is no dualistic distinction between the letter and the spirit, the Old Testament and the New Testament, and a single passage from its fuller meaning. After all, the deductive synthesis of Scripture afforded by the analogy of faith takes into account the resulting system of doctrine emerging from the whole of Scripture, which is the confessional Calvinist's "rule of faith and life." This respects both the human and divine dimensions of the Bible. In sum, we can always delve more deeply into a text of Scripture as long as we understand a text's meaning isn't marooned from the rest of the canon much less assume a necessary dualism of letter and spirit.

Our Lord states, "The words that I have spoken to you are spirit and life" (John 6:63 ESV). Moreover, He quotes, "'Man shall not live by bread alone, but by every word that proceeds from the mouth of God'" (Matthew 4:4). Every word of Scripture is spiritual and life-giving sustenance. Therefore, the quadriga as an interpretive framework or approach is a dualistic failure. Such dualism seeks to subvert and subordinate the "letter" to the "spirit." Ultimately, it lacks true virtue because it contradicts the Lord Jesus Himself. The words of Scripture are at once nothing more than literal and nothing less than spiritual.

As William Whitaker successfully argued, "For although the words may be applied and accommodated tropologically, allegorically, anagogically, or any other way; yet there are not therefore various senses, various interpretations and explications of Scripture, but there is but one sense, and that the literal, which may be variously accommodated, and from which various things may be collected."[13] The analogy of Scripture doesn't multiply senses. But it may multiply what genuinely follows from the single sense of scriptural words or passages rightly understood. This testifies to the superiority of the confessional Calvinist hermeneutic over the capricious and arbitrary medieval, premodern quadriga.

At an irreducible and foundational level, the quadriga must be refuted and allowed to collapse under the weight of its own irrationality and anti-Biblical dualism. The confessional Calvinist must be committed to a single-sense theory not only as a matter of historical precedent (it's in both the WCF and the 2LBCF) but also because Scripture does not separate the literal meaning of Scripture from other dimensions of meaning. The Calvinist confessions state that the sense of Scripture is one. When it comes to the Bible, then, the literal sense is the spiritual sense and vice-versa. So much for the quadriga and its attempted dualistic rehabilitation.

"Searched"

The interpreter's hermeneutical responsibility, whenever or wherever problems result from unclear texts, is to seek the

---

[13] William Whitaker, *Disputations on Holy Scripture* (Morgan, PA: Soli Deo Gloria Publications, 2000), 405.

resolution to such difficulties in other clearer portions of Scripture (analogy of Scripture). Sometimes the solution will be relatively simple. At other times the solution will be quite complex. It may involve extended observations, arguments, inferences, and deductions. In all these scenarios the resulting uniformity of scriptural doctrine (analogy of faith) only highlights all the more that the Bible is first and foremost not merely the words of men but also the very Word of God.

Sadly, certain theologians and teachers who should know better promote a concept of paradox as a legitimate hermeneutical category. They may say that since God is infinite, there is infinite meaning in the words of Scripture. Furthermore, some even maintain that because God is infinite, there are meanings and doctrines that are irreconcilable with each other in Scripture. Does this not militate against the validity of the analogy of Scripture and the analogy of faith? This sort of paradox, some maintain, is simply something we have to live with and relish due to our being finite creatures.

This is not the case at all. As a matter of fact, it is infinitely better (pun intended) not to speak of Scripture's meaning as infinite even if we attempt to base that on God's infinity. It is simply erroneous. The true and full sense of any Scripture is "not manifold but one." The fuller, deeper sense of Scripture entertains no contradictions or unresolvable paradoxes that interpreters must maintain to do supposed justice to both sides of conflicting texts or doctrines. Theologians, preachers, and teachers should be the first to search and harmonize questions about the true and full meaning of Scripture passages and doctrines.

It is inevitable that questions arise concerning the meaning of some scriptural text or other. However, the analogy of Scripture cries out to us to move beyond one's subjective paradox and not rest until we do the hard work of searching the Scriptures to arrive in objective territory. Paradox, which is relative to persons, should not be elevated to the position of a hermeneutical principle. After all, what is paradoxical to one person may not be paradoxical to another. Let the interpreter of Scripture never forget that portions of the Bible are not always clear in themselves "nor alike clear unto all." Interpreters should never ascribe their intellectual limitations onto others. That would be arrogance, not piety. Paradox in hermeneutics can lead only to paradox in exegesis.

"Known"

Furthermore, as we do compare Scripture with Scripture (analogy of Scripture), we accumulate biblical evidence. Implications are validly drawn out, possible interpretations are eliminated, and control beliefs are modified and subjugated to the truth of God's Word. Because Scripture cannot be broken (John 10:35), what emerges as texts supplement texts in a holistic, systematic fashion is a uniformity of teaching. The analogy of faith cries out to us to reach for the baton of well-established and judiciously arrived-at doctrine and continue running the race.

Consider the following example. Scripture teaches that God is one and indivisible. Scripture also teaches that in the "unity of the Godhead there be three persons, of one substance, power, and eternity" (WCF, chapter 2, section

3). If interpreters had stopped comparing Scripture with Scripture and simply held that God was one with three modes of existence (modalism), where would biblical Trinitarianism be? No, method always matters. The early church councils didn't merely conclude, "This is paradoxical. The Scriptures underdetermine whether God is one in one sense and three in a different sense. Because of the infinity of God, let us hold to God as one and God as three in the same sense in tension!"

Athanasius must always prevail over Arius!

4. The Unity and Diversity of Scripture

The fourth and final interlocking link in the chain of foundational hermeneutical assumptions is the unity and diversity of Holy Writ. The Bible is not, despite what unbelievers say, a mishmash of contradictory fables. Definite unity is rightly perceptible throughout its diverse pages.

There is a discernible cohesion in the midst of the diverse texts within Scripture. In fact, what emerges for the responsible interpreter as he applies "a due use of the ordinary means" to the Bible is what the Westminster Confession says is "the consent of all the parts" (chapter 1, section 5).

There are two ways we can apprehend the unity and diversity of Scripture. One way is through the *history of redemption* (also known as biblical theology). The other way is through *systematic theology*. The former focuses on the chronological unfolding of God's revelation to His people in history as recorded in Scripture. The latter focuses on the logical ordering of scriptural revelation into a system of doctrines.

These work together as bifocal lenses, allowing the interpreter to appreciate both the redemptive-historical forest and the systematic theological trees, neither at the expense of the other. In fact, roughly speaking, biblical theology traverses the history of redemption via the analogy of Scripture while systematic theology views each of the parts of Scripture via "the general tenor of God's Word" according to the analogy of faith (i.e., the system of orthodox doctrines that can also be referred to as the whole counsel of God per Acts 20:27).

This book can only scratch the surface concerning the organic unity found within the diversity of God's Word. Consider the history of redemption. Scripture wonderfully and dramatically displays its organic and progressive unfolding, much as the planted bulb emerges from the ground as a growing bud and in the fullness of time blossoms into a beautiful tulip! The tulip can no more disparage the bulb than systematic theology can disparage biblical theology—or vice-versa.

To use another figurative illustration, "[All] the books of the Bible have their binding center in Jesus Christ. They all relate to the work of redemption and the founding of God's kingdom on earth."[14] Thus, just as the pages of your Bible make contact with and are held together at the spine with adhesive or stitches, so Christ-centered meaning permeates and holds together the various Christ-ward meanings throughout the pages of God's Word no matter where you turn the page.

In fact, according to our Lord and Savior Himself, the Old Testament set the stage book by book, epoch by epoch, covenant by covenant, and promise by promise to point

---

14 Berkhof, *Principles*, 53.

forward in some way, shape, or form to the Savior's glorious work of redemption for His people. See the following passages:

> Then He said to them, "O foolish ones, and slow of heart to believe in all that the prophets have spoken! Ought not the Christ to have suffered these things and to enter into His glory?" And beginning at Moses and all the Prophets, He expounded to them in all the Scriptures the things concerning Himself. . . . Then He said to them, "These are the words which I spoke to you while I was still with you, that all things must be fulfilled which were written in the Law of Moses and the Prophets and the Psalms concerning Me." And He opened their understanding, that they might comprehend the Scriptures. Then He said to them, "Thus it is written, and thus it was necessary for the Christ to suffer and to rise from the dead the third day, and that repentance and remission of sins should be preached in His name to all nations, beginning at Jerusalem." (Luke 24:25–27, 44–47)

> "But those things which God foretold by the mouth of all His prophets, that the Christ would suffer, He has thus fulfilled. . . . whom heaven must receive until the times of restoration of all things, which God has spoken by the mouth of all His holy prophets since the world began. . . . Yes, and all the prophets, from Samuel and those who follow, as many as have spoken, have also foretold these days." (Acts 3:18, 21, 24)

Then Paul, as his custom was, went in to them, and for three Sabbaths reasoned with them from the Scriptures, explaining and demonstrating that the Christ had to suffer and rise again from the dead, and saying, "This Jesus whom I preach to you is the Christ." (Acts 17:2–3)

"I stand, witnessing both to small and great, saying no other things than those which the prophets and Moses said would come—that the Christ would suffer, that He would be the first to rise from the dead, and would proclaim light to the Jewish people and to the Gentiles." (Acts 26:22–23)

Of this salvation the prophets have inquired and searched carefully, who prophesied of the grace that would come to you, searching what, or what manner of time, the Spirit of Christ who was in them was indicating when He testified beforehand the sufferings of Christ and the glories that would follow. (1 Peter 1:10–11)

The Old Testament was not a Christless revelation. Quite the contrary. By means of definite plot points, messianic prophecies, figures, types, shadows, and other details, we can rightly understand God drawing His people's gaze unavoidably to Christ as powerfully in the Old Testament as in the New Testament. As Mark Garcia has stated, the text of Scripture, including the Old Testament, is "drawing us by the gravitational pull of Christ Himself into the world given to us in Christ to live in that world, to metabolize these words which are the bread of life to us, to draw us deeper into faith, hope, and love."[15] The Old Testament is nothing if not the Christ-centered preparation for the Christological fullness of the New Testament.

The New Testament is nothing if not the fulfillment and climactic inauguration of God's promised redemptive purpose in Christ. The fully-orbed significance of Christ's person and the work He accomplished at Calvary is what the New Testament explains and exults over. It is the central theme of worship in the New Testament. The Scriptures of the Old and New Testament alone are the words of Christ. The words of Christ are the means by which Christ is formed in us. This is, as Mark Garcia has said, "more than a captivating idea; it's a captivating life."[16]

The multifaceted and systematic implications of our Lord's person and work reach out backwards to Old Testament saints and forward to us. The glory of God in Christ is the new song belonging to the people of God because we have been reconciled to God and each other by God's grace. All of Scripture, whether in Christ-ward promise or Christ-centered fulfillment, details the defeat of evil in all its forms in Christ, by Christ, and through Christ.

This is the warp and woof of confessional Calvinist biblical interpretation. Berkof, for example, observed,

---

15   Mark Garcia, "Constructing the Cosmos, the Woman, the Glory: Proverbs 31 Reconsidered," July 8, 2021, in *Greystone Conversations*, produced by Greystone Theological Institute, podcast, 59:59, https://podcasts.apple.com/us/podcast/greystone-conversations/id1518156157?i=1000528203521.
16   Garcia, "Constructing the Cosmos, the Woman, the Glory: Proverbs 31 Reconsidered," 1:00:34.

[M]any of the Old Testament types pointed ultimately to the New Testament realities; many prophecies found their final fulfillment in Jesus Christ, no matter how many of the Psalms give utterance to the joy and sorrow, not merely of the poets, but of the people of God as a whole, and, in some cases, of the suffering and triumphant Messiah. These considerations lead us to what may be called, the deeper sense of Scripture.[17]

But they do so by comparing Scripture with Scripture, accumulating and synthesizing biblical evidence, and drawing out valid implications. Texts supplement texts (analogy of Scripture). Uniformity in teachings (analogy of faith) is reached precisely because of a non-arbitrary, non-capricious, proper, and rational method of biblical interpretation. This whole lifelong process is also the warp and woof that delivers to us the fortunes of a Reformed worldview!

In sum, the Scriptures display, despite their diversity, a glorious unity of content. Whether it is the individual biblical books, doctrines, concepts, motifs, themes, covenants, promises, failures, fulfillments, genres, authors, or ultimately, the transcendent, lofty God of holiness who is mighty and merciful to save man from his miserable plight, we have no right to conclude that the Bible is a disparate collection of writings. It is folly to actively seek to unfasten New Testament Christianity from the Old Testament. Why? Because as Reformed philosopher James Anderson has stated, "If you unhitch Christianity from the Old Testament, you'll eventually

---

[17] Berkhof, *Principles*, 60.

unhitch Christianity from Christ, because Christ hitched himself to the Old Testament."[18]

We are indispensably helped along the way to apprehend Scripture's organic unity by means of both biblical theology and systematic theology. Scripture itself marries Christ-centered, overarching "meaning" with Christ-ward "meanings," text with text and testament with testament, thus showing that God Himself has joined unity with diversity. Therefore, what God has joined together let no interpreter tear asunder.

Suggested Reading Strategies for Understanding Sacred Scripture

To understand the meaning of a Scripture text, you have to apply your thinking process to the thinking process of the Scripture's authors (especially its ultimate divine Author). The reader of Scripture can grasp its meaning only as he appreciates more and more the style, content, and conventions of communication embedded in the text. Why? Because God revealed His Word through human authors in time-and-space history as He was dealing with His people in specific circumstances. We don't seek to penetrate through the text to something beyond the words and propositions of Scripture, because God's special revelation is the words and propositions that comprise the text of Scripture itself. "Sanctify them by Your truth. Your word is truth" (John 17:17), said the Lord Jesus. All meaning is found in the text, not behind or beyond it.

---

18   Originally posted on X, formerly Twitter, by Dr. James N. Anderson (@proginosko) on October 5, 2023, at 12:56 p.m.

That is how a reader gets at the thinking process of the biblical authors and Scripture's ultimate divine Author: whatever is explicitly or implicitly drawn from the text, given its features and affordances rightly understood, is what the authors and the Author intended to communicate. The reader must be ready to engage with the text on its own terms—the terms dictated by its authors and its Author. Careful, close, and mindful attention to the text is the only option for the confessional Calvinist as a matter of biblical commitment and conviction. The psalmist reminds us, "You have magnified Your word above all Your name" (Psalm 138:2). This is how God's people hear His voice.

First we must examine the appropriately chosen text by a close, attentive, mindful, and repeated reading of the passage. An appropriate text basically means a cohesive unit of thought between a sentence and a paragraph in length. The length of the text will usually depend on the genre it is part of in Scripture.

For example, in a narrative portion of the Bible, a prolonged prose passage of many paragraphs can be divided into many parts that communicate various streams of thought, episodes of life involving people and events, that contribute to its overall flow. Prose lends itself to the qualities of narratives. Whether it is personal narratives (e.g., the story of Abraham), familial narratives (e.g., the story of Jacob and his sons), or national narratives (e.g., the story of Israel during its united kingdom period), they all share certain qualities that prominently convey truth through the stories of people, places, events, conflicts, failures, and triumphs.

However, in distinction from prose of narrative, the Bible also employs the vehicle of poetry to convey its thoughts and truth. The Psalms, for example, are lyrical expressions of praise, celebration, lament, complaint, and even the depths of despair. These passages contain more abbreviated and concentrated units of thought. Yet for all their brevity and pithiness, they lack nothing in profundity, significance, immanence, transcendence, and applicability to the reader.

So then, a close and attentive reading of an appropriately chosen biblical text involves a dissatisfaction with a merely cursory reading. It involves a deep dissatisfaction with a superficial comprehension of the biblical text. Close and attentive reading means being as mindful of the emergence of meaning from scriptural revelation as an expectant mother is of giving birth to her baby. A mother spends nine months monitoring closely the progress of her pregnancy. She eats properly. She adapts to the nausea in the early months by eating strategically to keep food down. She has regular and frequent doctor visits for ultrasounds and blood tests. On the day of delivery, a myriad of measures are in place to assure a safe and successful delivery for both mother and child. Similarly, a responsible reader is a serious reader who closely monitors his or her comprehension of the text according to the text itself.

What is a close reading of the Bible mindful of? It is mindful of not imposing meaning on the text. It is mindful of the text's content, structure, function, context, integration with other Scripture texts (especially with Christological significance), and gleaning ideas and conclusions only from the text itself. A close and attentive reading of the Bible is a strategy that seeks to yield evidence-based deductions from an analysis of the content and particulars of the text itself.

The success of this strategy is improved by repeated readings and enhanced by thinking about the details of the text along the continuum of revelation of the person, work, and offices of the Lord Jesus. After all, in addition to not imposing meaning onto a text, the mindful reader should not unduly close off a particular text to its integration with the rest of the Christological significance of Scripture. No text of Scripture is an island unto itself. No meaning of any particular text of Scripture is marooned from the rest of Scripture.

Second, examine the flow of thought displayed in the chosen passage itself as well as how it functionally fits within its surrounding literary context. For example, if your chosen text is a sentence or two, how does it fit within the paragraph? If your chosen text is a paragraph, how does it fit within its larger surrounding context?

Regardless of the length of the text under consideration, the reader's examination will have to include a text's use of language, the function of its grammar, special terms, patterns of organization, figures of speech, and other similar issues. Again, these are usually dependent on the genre the text is a part of in Scripture.

Beyond these immediate literary contextual considerations, the reader must always be willing to take notice of broader thematic considerations throughout the canon of Scripture. As stated above, no passage of Scripture is an island unto itself nor is the meaning of any particular text of Scripture marooned from the rest of Scripture. Among the greatest theological themes in the Bible is how God commenced, continued, and culminated His redemptive work in Christ. From its announcement to its fulfillment in the Old and New Testaments, respectively, the careful reader and interpreter will integrate the various meanings of the biblical books in each testament with the overarching meaning of the Christ who wrought salvation along redemptive-historical lines as the chain of islands of an archipelago.

What is the bottom line? No matter how many foundational hermeneutical assumptions and the interpretive reading strategies that flow from them there are, the bottom line is this, as Augustine one day heard a group of children sing while playing: *Take up and read!* All believers, including confessional Calvinists, can heartily agree with that. What lies next for all of us is simply to take up our Bibles and read! By doing so, we will be attending to the voice of God by attending to what the Scripture says.

To conclude, the true confessional Calvinist interpreter of Scripture is neither a butcher of the biblical text nor a naive and superficial biblicist. The confessional Calvinist follows the biblical example of the Bereans and the wise counsel of William Hendricksen by becoming "thoroughly acquainted" with the Bible by "reading the Bible itself. Read not a small portion but a book at a time; say, Genesis in its entirety. What next? Read it again! At least three times! Get into the spirit of the book! See the Christ revealed in it!"[19]

---

19 William Hendricksen, *Survey of the Bible* (Grand Rapids, MI: Baker Books, 1995), 43.

Part 2:

The Warrior

Gird Your sword upon Your thigh, O Mighty One,
With Your glory and Your majesty.
And in Your majesty ride prosperously
because of truth, humility, and righteousness;
And Your right hand shall teach
You awesome things.
(Psalm 45:3–4)

Chapter 3:
Zion and David?

A wise man scales the city of the mighty, and brings down the trusted stronghold.

(Proverbs 21:22)

What are we to make of William Hendricksen's counsel to see the Christ revealed in Genesis? He says that believers should get into the spirit of Genesis and unashamedly declares that Christ is revealed therein. Whereas in practice many churches seem to unofficially rely upon a "canon within a canon," usually a portion of the New Testament preachers turn to because its content is explicitly Christian, Hendricksen seems to imply that we haven't plumbed the depths of meaning in Genesis until we draw from its Christological significance. Hendricksen is correct. Genesis, along with the rest of the Old Testament, is just as Christian as the New Testament. This axiomatic truth is confirmed through a myriad of internal principles and reading strategies that fit as solidly together as a Roman arch.

Perhaps it would not be amiss to draw an analogy from the art world again. There is an artistic technique called the "mirror anamorphosis." For our purposes, imagine we have a painting of a mountain range with a valley in the middle. The mirror anamorphosis requires placing a cylindrical mirror in the center of the valley between the mountain range to reveal a further image in the reflection of what is objectively there in the mountain range by design. This can illustrate by analogy how the full range of biblical data unites in Christocentric reflection to reveal what is objectively there by design in both testaments of the Bible.

Now, this is not to say that this reading process is simple. Painting is one thing. Interpreting Scripture is another. However, let's engage the Old Testament through fearless Christocentrism. On a difficulty scale for a redemptive-historical preaching text, 2 Samuel 5:6–10 would be scored moderate or high. This passage details David's conquest of Jerusalem and the siege at Zion that established David as the undisputed warrior king of God's covenant people, Israel. The Christocentric difficulty score for this passage is no walk in the park. But it could be what some old-school Dutch Reformed believers referred to in the days of way back as "a bicycle ride through the Bible."

Redemptive-historical teaching and preaching are like a bike ride through the Bible because you experience being transported from point A to point B. Not exhaustively, but sufficiently to convey the sermon's point. Everything about the journey is important. The right starting point and end point guarantee that you are on the right journey. The journey involves determining the communicative intent of 2 Samuel 5:6–10.

At a time when my pastor asked me to preach for an upcoming the Lord's Supper service, I was reading a fascinating book concerning Reformed biblical interpretation and preaching.[20] The author discussed a sermon by Korean seminary professor and pastor Dr. Won-Tae Suk, "The Redemptive-Historical Implication of Recapturing Zion," based on 2 Samuel 5:6–10. I was intrigued and stimulated by that title and the text. Dr. Yung Hoon-Hyun writes,

> Suk described first the historical and literary context of David's recapturing of Zion through examining scriptural texts before and after the event, and then explained that Zion symbolized the Old Testament Church, and then explained that the New Testament also adopted this name. Finally, just as David recaptured Zion the fortress and made it God's dwelling place, Christ also recaptured his people from the enemy to form his church.[21]

David's Conquest of Jerusalem

Can you see why I was intrigued? I think that all preachers and teachers should find this approach to the passage thoroughly fascinating. Indeed, any reader of Scripture should be intrigued.

---

20 Yung Hoon Hyun, *Redemptive-Historical Hermeneutics and Homiletics: Debates in Holland, America, and Korea from 1930–2012* (Eugene, OR: Wipf & Stock, 2015), 260–87.
21 Hyun, *Redemptive-Historical Hermeneutics and Homiletics*, 275.

What, then, would be a right starting point for a right reading of Scripture? We can begin our journey in broad terms by analyzing the text's literary and historical content and context. As we go along on this journey, we will see how appropriate it may be to allow the canonical context to inform our reading of this passage. After all, there is the Calvinistic hermeneutical principle that no text of Scripture is an island unto itself. Scripture interprets, enriches, enhances, augments, supplements, complements, and aggrandizes Scripture via the analogy of Scripture and the analogy of faith. Scripture does a similar work on the interpreter as well. The question is, Does 2 Samuel 5:6–10 lend itself to a fully-orbed analysis that results in a legitimately Christocentric synthesis? Dr. Suk certainly believed so. After considering the verses he cites as evidence, so do I.

The passage says,

> And the king and his men went to Jerusalem against the Jebusites, the inhabitants of the land, who spoke to David, saying, "You shall not come in here; but the blind and the lame will repel you," thinking, "David cannot come in here." Nevertheless David took the stronghold of Zion (that is, the City of David). Now David said on that day, "Whoever climbs up by way of the water shaft and defeats the Jebusites (the lame and the blind, who are hated by David's soul), he shall be chief and captain." Therefore they say, "The blind and the lame shall not come into the house." Then David dwelt in the stronghold, and called

it the City of David. And David built all around from the Millo and inward. So David went on and became great, and the Lord God of hosts was with him.

THE LITERARY AND HISTORICAL CONTEXTS

The literary context of 2 Samuel 5:6–10 comprises what immediately surrounds this passage. Verses 1–4 detail Israel's tribal leaders unifying under David's rule and his anointing by them to officially inaugurate his reign. Verses 11–25 complete chapter 5 and show how David's influence was strengthened and expanded. He received gifts from one foreign kingdom, Tyre, while receiving the Lord's blessing to defeat another foreign kingdom, that of the Philistines.

The historical context includes the fact that this is Israel's "Monarchy 2.0," so to speak. King Saul suffered a mortal physical wound on the field of battle long after suffering a mortal spiritual wound of pride, disobedience, and rebellion against God. The monarchy so desired by the people of Israel was a failure, both temporally and spiritually. Remember—it came about only because the Israelites wanted a king so they could be like the other nations. Their request represented a direct affront to God, and that evaluation was from God Himself. But in spite of this unfaithfulness, the sin of rejecting God's kingship, God consistently showed that He would be faithful. Moreover, no such effort can dethrone God. He stands revealed as the matchless Monarch and His grace would reign all the more supreme. These are the circumstances under which David became king.

For all his faults, David wanted his throne to be aligned and eventually identified with God's throne. Reformed biblical scholar O. P. Robertson rightly observed, "All along, David seems to have envisioned the merger of his throne with God's throne. He intended to build a house for his God at the capital city of his kingdom (2 Samuel 7:1–3)."[22]

We must conclude that for literary and historical contextual reasons, the section we are dealing with may suggest deeper significance than what surface-level considerations can yield. But note well: to say that this or any passage of Scripture has a deeper meaning does not denote a dual meaning, and much less, an arbitrary and capricious quadruple meaning of Scripture. A right reading of Scripture does not bifurcate a literal sense from a spiritual sense. Much less does a right reading of Scripture multiply the sense of Scripture into four capricious and arbitrary compartments.

THE SENSUS PLENIOR

On the other hand, neither is the sense of Scripture exhausted by its grammatical and historical facts. The right reading of Scripture acknowledges that the literal is the spiritual, and the single sense is the *sensus plenior*.

Dr. Suk indicates in the title of his sermon how he chooses to proceed. He uses a redemptive-historical approach to yield the deeper, not dual or quadruple, meaning of this seminal passage. Since I don't have the content of his sermon, however, I am in the dark about how he developed his message, but not

---

[22] O. Palmer Robertson, *Understanding the Land of the Bible: A Biblical-Theological Guide* (Phillipsburg, NJ: P & R Publishing, 1996), 98.

in total darkness. The redemptive-historical approach seeks to go beyond a superficial understanding of the text and follow the organic development of scriptural revelation to track and follow the unfolding of how both the biblical authors and the divine Author used a person, place, event, and such to unveil a fuller picture of the truth.

Now let us move forward and not be satisfied with either superficiality or ivory-tower theories of interpretation. I would like for us to get our hands dirty. Always have your Bible at the ready. Keep it right next to you. Because this passage is part of the narrative genre, we can begin observing and provisionally analyzing its textual structure along the lines of its chronological order as an entryway for analysis.

The story of David taking Jerusalem and the siege at Zion has a beginning, a middle, and an end. King David and his men went to Jerusalem after his anointing by the unified elders of Israel. David and company were met with opposition from the Jebusites, who inhabited Jerusalem and expressed arrogant confidence in their stronghold at Zion. David pronounced a determined mental purpose to obliterate their opposition, owing to a deep hatred for them. He specified how Israel would defeat the Jebusites, and the final result was complete victory. According to the text, David became greater and greater because the Lord of hosts was with him.

It's a very straightforward account. This passage describes a cast of characters brought together in a city in which a sequence of events takes place. Action ensues. Readers may use the affordance of the sequence of events to formulate a basic provisional outline. Yours may be different. (1) David came. (2) David saw. (3) David conquered. A good working title could be simply "David's Conquest of Jerusalem and Zion." We can fill in the details relevant to this passage by asking and answering some questions.

1. DAVID CAME.

What was the setting in which the events took place? David came to Jerusalem, that ancient city known and inhabited by various groups of people since the days of Genesis, known variously as Salem, Jerusalem, and even Jebus, because the Jebusites were the latest pagan people to dwell there. Despite the fact that Jerusalem was given to the tribe of Benjamin [see Joshua 18:28 and Judges 1:21], from which King Saul originated, the tribe never conquered it. It was very much under the Jebusites' control. This makes David's confrontation that much more momentous.

The contest is one of David's audacity versus the Jebusites' arrogance. He was not content with containing them. Conquest was the only option. The Jebusites weren't innocent victims of Israel's dreams of expansion. They were not neutral parties with whom reason could prevail. These were recalcitrant rebels against God, who occupied land that did not belong to them. They were on holy ground, defiling it and defying the anointed king. They willfully ignored that payday would come someday, and they were prepared to insolently do battle to the last man. They said as much. As a prelude to actual battle, they verbally battled and directed their taunts towards David, saying, "You shall not come in here, but the blind and the lame will repel you." Their words matched their thoughts in perfect harmony because they were defiantly convinced: David cannot come in here.

The question arises: Who are "the blind and the lame" referred to by the Jebusites? Whoever they are, these lame and blind seem to be special objects of David's hatred. Verse 8 says that "the lame and the blind [were] hated by David's soul." It was widely known that no blind or lame would enter or dwell in his house. The scene is set before us with two determinations juxtaposed: the Jebusites' determination to repel King David's siege, expressed in their taunt "the blind and the lame will repel you," and David's determination to attack and eliminate them. As the chiastic structure of the text emphasizes, the stakes were whether Jerusalem would be made the capital of the united kingdom of Israel as the City of David.

Either the blind and the lame would prevail for the Jebusites, or they would be defeated by David's command. Whose determinations and aspirations will be fulfilled? Whose city and fortress are they? Herein lies a difficulty in understanding what is meant by "the blind and the lame."

The Jebusites were the first to mention the blind and the lame. David either takes for granted their meaning and adopts it, or he uses the terms with a different meaning. The Jebusites were clearly defiant. They saw Israel's defeat and loss of King Saul at the hands of the Philistines. To lose Jerusalem and Zion seemed unthinkable to them. They firmly believed their mouths could write checks that their backsides could cash. That last sentence is a figure of speech. So is the phrase "the blind and the lame." In the mouths of the Jebusites, this was an intentional verbal reproach against David, whose people were on a losing streak. Israel's God was surely being bested by the Philistines' gods, and now the Jebusites and their deities would have their turn.

This Jebusite figure of speech signified a taunt precisely because it was a verbal reproach against David as a perceived weakened opponent—so weak that even the blind and the lame Jebusite soldiers (a hyperbolic idiom) would be able to repel his attack.

How does David respond? Does he magnanimously absorb the reproach as a noble, newly anointed king? David hears what they're saying loud and clear. He is, after all, a poet. Without hesitation, this warrior poet, at least mentally, declares his determination and his hatred for their blind and lame. In fact, these blind and lame can get it first. And once victory is achieved, he never wants to see any blind or lame ever again, much less in his own home or palace. As much as the Jebusites hated David, David reciprocated, and there's no denying he specifically targeted the blind and the lame. The question is—Did David feel obligated to stick with their specific take—their *usus loquendi* (common speaking usage of the time) of a hyperbolic idiom? If so, David was simply expressing a particularly focused hatred toward Jebusite soldiers who were disabled. That would be a literalistic response to their figurative reproach.

Another possibility is that David was employing a synecdoche on the spot meant to imply that since their initial mention of the blind and the lame was a reproach to him, he would use the same phrase as an expression of "the part for the whole" to return their reproach. In this case, as much as

David's ire was directed at the blind and the lame disabled soldiers, he would certainly exercise all his might against the whole Jebusite fighting force.

In the case of these two interpretive options, David was either simply expressing his hatred toward disabled veterans, because he was simply "that kind of guy," or he was employing a particular figure of speech against the Jebusites as a whole while only mentioning the part. Would it be reasonable to conclude that he never countenanced any of his own mighty men for suffering incapacitating injuries in the fields of battle who previously fought alongside him? Must the contemporary reader be satisfied with such a literalistic interpretation? More likely David meant to imply that since their initial mention of the blind and the lame was a reproach to him, he would use the same phrase as a synecdoche, an expression of "the part for the whole" to return their reproach. Perhaps he used "the blind and the lame" to dismiss the entire Jebusite army.

Parenthetically, some interpreters demur at David's seeming disparagement of disabled people. They lazily take the erroneous route of labeling David as an "ableist" for his hatred of the blind and the lame. But there are contextual reasons for not going this route that shed light on the most likely correct reading of this challenging passage.

I want to suggest an additional possibility beyond the conventional interpretations of the wordplay. David does not operate under the obligation to use "the blind and the lame" the same way the Jebusites did. Neither should the reader. "The blind and the lame" here refers not to actual disabled people but to idols or statues. For all his faults, David never turned to idolatry, which was the besetting sin of much of Israel. On the other hand, idolatry and the worship of statues held great appeal to the Jebusites and was the warp and woof of their existence. They expressed total confidence in their deities strategically placed along Zion's walls to prevent anyone, including David, from successfully seizing it. As much as David understood their initial taunting reproach of him, they heard what David was saying loud and clear as well. David's hatred for the Jebusites' lame and blind idols was religious at its core. Despite knowing that the statues could neither walk nor see, the Jebusites placed their faith in these lame and blind objects for victory over the nation whose God was the Lord Almighty. Such is the blindness of sin. For this reason David would not even entrust their presence as a trophy of victory in his palace once the siege was successful. "The blind and the lame shall not come into the house."

Psalm 115 is an appropriate and directly applicable supplementary text to highlight the foundational religious undertones of the contest between Israel, led by David, and the Jebusites, led by "the blind and the lame." It says in part (vv. 2–8)—

> Why should the Gentiles say,
> "So where is their God?"
> But our God is in heaven;
> He does whatever He pleases.
> Their idols are silver and gold,
> The work of men's hands.
> They have mouths, but they do not speak;

> Eyes they have, but they do not see;
> They have ears, but they do not hear;
> Noses they have, but they do not smell;
> They have hands, but they do not handle;
> Feet they have, but they do not walk;
> Nor do they mutter through their throat.
> Those who make them are like them;
> So is everyone who trusts in them.[23]

Further confirmation of this reading is found a little later, in 2 Samuel 9:3. In a most touching kingly scene, we find David looking for and finding a member of Saul's family to show him kindness for Jonathan's sake. It so happened that Jonathan left behind a son, Mephibosheth. In escaping with haste at the news of King Saul's and Jonathan's death, his caregiver dropped the boy, who was permanently injured and became lame in both feet (2 Samuel 4:4). Nevertheless, King David decreed that he "shall eat bread at my table always" (2 Samuel 9:10) as one of the king's sons, despite being lame in both his feet. Therefore, clearly David did not actually express hatred for blind and lame people in his disdain for Jebusites. And so we continue.

2. DAVID SAW.

We have seen the cast of characters brought together in a particular place. David's gaze was now set to put his audacity into action. He was a military strategist and tactician. The objective was not to contain but to conquer the stronghold

---

[23] See also Isaiah 41:21–25; 44:9–20.

of Zion. It was time to cash that Jebusite check, and King David was the currency exchange. What did David see that could be done against the Jebusites? After all, the battle for Zion would be an actual uphill battle, with the further aggravating requirement to breach the stronghold's walls. This was no cakewalk. Although the Jebusites' idolatry was irrational, their arrogant confidence in Zion's structure is at least understandable. The fortress seemed impregnable.

This is the first recorded mention of Zion in the Bible but most certainly not the last. As anyone can see by a perusal through the references in a reference or study Bible, Zion is subsequently used throughout the rest of Scripture to denote the temple area and especially God's personal capital and site of His earthly kingdom.

It's as if Zion became paradigmatic for more than just a fortress conquered by King David. Dr. Suk capitalized on this biblical usage to enhance our understanding of David's conquest of Zion in 2 Samuel 5. Was he being an irresponsible reader of Scripture and importing future uses of Zion back into 2 Samuel 5? The biblical authors were not irresponsible writers in employing Zion to signify deeper, but not dual, meaning beyond the superficial significance of the physical fortress in Jerusalem. More pointedly, the Holy Spirit was not wrong to inspire the use of the term *Zion* to signify a deeper, but not dual, truth regarding the meaning of Zion's conquest for all of God's people.

It seems to me that when Scripture uses *Zion* in a paradigmatic fashion, readers and interpreters should pay attention. We must not unduly close off the boundaries of meaning by a superficial grammatical-historical interpretation of Scripture. We must be audacious readers when the Spirit has been an audacious inspirer. But we must never be arrogant in ignoring the deeper, not dual, meaning that Scripture itself speaks of repeatedly. *Zion* is one example. It lends itself naturally, from the text of Scripture, to digging more deeply than with a superficial or isolated notion of the historical sense.

A surface-level grammatical-historical significance in no way exhausts a text's single *sensus plenior*. All things considered, in the case of David's conquest of Zion we can go so far as to say that it is an integrative motif that serves the people of God as a major redemptive-historical marker as they take their bicycle ride through the Bible. This is no ivory tower, keep-your-hands-clean, academic theory of hermeneutics.

Let's consider some of the verses relevant to how various biblical authors, including King David himself, use *Zion* later in Scripture. We're just scratching the surface here. Let's sample some verses.

- "The tribe of your inheritance . . . This Mount Zion, where You have dwelt" (Psalm 74:2).
- "Of Zion it will be said, 'This one and that one were born in her'" (Psalm 87:5).
- "Mercy on Zion" (Psalm 102:13).
- "Bless you out of Zion. . . . the good of Jerusalem" (Psalm 128:5).
- "The Lord has chosen Zion. He desired it for His dwelling place. . . . There I will make the horn of David grow" (Psalm 132:13, 17).

- "Descending upon the mountains of Zion; For there the Lord commanded the blessing—Life forevermore" (Psalm 133:3).
- "And say to Zion, 'You are My people'" (Isaiah 51:16).

Do you see how taking the literal features of these verses, namely the synecdoches and the metonymies made from Zion, draws our gaze to a paradigmatic aspect of the significance of Zion?

Let's continue.

- "The Deliverer will come out of Zion" (Romans 11:26).
- "The Jerusalem above is free, which is the mother of us all" (Galatians 4:26—personification there).
- "You have come to Mount Zion and to the city of the living God, the heavenly Jerusalem" (Hebrews 12:22).
- "I lay in Zion a chief cornerstone" (1 Peter 2:6—you know who that is: the Lord Jesus).
- "A lamb standing on Mount Zion" (Revelation 14:1).

As we can all see by a perusal of subsequent passages by a figure of speech, including some by King David himself, the historical event of the conquest of Zion was so significant that it served as a paradigmatic symbol for the people of God—the place where God dwelt in the midst of His people, and as a poetic and typological description of the Old Testament church. Moreover, not only the Old Testament church but also the New Testament representation of the church and its spiritual identity.

Zion can be taken for the people who lived there and continue to live there, not physically but spiritually, not the Jebusites, not exclusively the ancient Israelites but the people of God in all ages. As with the Exodus event, the acquisition of Jerusalem and the conquest of the stronghold of Zion were a big deal that was destined to become permanently paradigmatic for God's acquisition of a redeemed people. That is precisely how it is used in the rest of the Old Testament, and it is carried over in the New Testament by the apostles to refer to Christians without hesitation or apology.

Chapter 4:
Brief Excursus Concerning Zion

"In strategy, it is important to see distant things as if they were close and to take a distanced view of close things."

(Miyamoto Musashi, *Book of Five Rings*)

A brief excursus is in order before we continue. We chose to emphasize *Zion* as an integrating motif because it is frequently used as such by other authors and passages in the Old Testament and is further expanded in the New Testament. This usage supports having a notion of a deeper or fuller meaning of Scripture—a deeper, not a dual or an arbitrarily quadruple, medieval multiplicity of meanings. Dual authorship, yes—the human and the divine. Double or quadruple meanings? No. Both the Westminster Confession of Faith and the Second London Baptist Confession of Faith explicitly state that the true and the full sense of any Scripture is one. They explicitly deny a manifold sense, which of necessity includes the arbitrary and capricious fourfold sense of the quadriga.

Scripture's single sense is an axiomatic necessity of thought and speech. The signers and framers of the confessions took this for granted. Why? For the simple reason that to assert a dual or quadruple sense would be tantamount to allowing arbitrary and capricious boundaries to determine meaning and thus would make communication uncertain and irrational. In fact, there are myriad historical examples of very fanciful, interpretive conclusions by the church's medieval scholars that privilege the clever interpreter rather than the holy Text. So, it cannot be simply a matter of an abusive use of the quadriga as a method of interpretation. The problem is that the method itself is irredeemably illegitimate. One thing is for sure: to be deep in the history of Biblical interpretation is to cease to be quadrigal.

Note well, though, the single sense is not limited to superficial notions of lexicography, semantics, grammar, history, and such, as important as they are. Why assume that? Both the Westminster Confession of Faith and the Second London Baptist Confession of Faith confess that Scripture is pregnant with meaning. No text is an island unto itself. In fact, both confessions are explicit. They say, "When there is a question about the true and full sense of any Scripture, which is not manifold, but one, it must be searched out and known by other places that speak more clearly." Meaning in Scripture is not marooned.

This is precisely what we try to model with the interpretive issues in the use of "the blind and the lame" and "Zion" in 2

Samuel 5:6–10. Meaning is singular, but it contains a figure of speech and a play on words in the former, along with the introduction of an integrating theological motif or typology in the latter. Whatever we call it, it is a textual feature and reality of Scripture that is confirmed by good and necessary consequence from Scripture. This can be done either explicitly or implicitly. The single sense of Scripture, therefore, is in no way limited to superficial notions of the grammatical-historical meaning.

In fact, leaving things at a superficial grammatical-historical level may not yield even a correct understanding at all, as consideration of "the blind and the lame" demonstrates. We must not unduly isolate what God in Scripture did not intend for us to isolate. More often than we may think, there is a deeper, not quadruple, meaning behind the surface. On one occasion the Lord Jesus asked His disciples, "'Have you understood all these things?' They said to him, 'Yes, Lord.' Then He said to them, "Therefore every scribe instructed concerning the kingdom of heaven is like a householder who brings out of his treasure things new and old" (Matthew 13:51–52). Matthew Henry observed that "truths mutually explain and illustrate one another."[24] And the Bible, my friends, is our treasure of truth.

It seems uncontroversial and almost a trivial point to emphasize that there exists a deeper, albeit single, *sensus plenior* in Holy Scripture. What is *sensus plenior*? Let's start with what it is not. *Sensus plenior* is not infinite, manifold,

---

[24] Matthew Henry, *Matthew Henry's Commentary on the Whole Bible* (Peabody, MA: Hendrickson Publishers, 1991), 1682.

quadruple, or even a double meaning in Scripture. Neither is it a supposed emergent meaning felt by the reader as he or she reflects on his or her life's experience in light of Scripture. That's just subjectivism. *Sensus plenior* simply refers to the fact that the meaning of Scripture can be enhanced, supplemented, augmented, and enriched beyond a surface-level understanding of what the human author of a text of Scripture intended. Whether the human author intended something deeper at the time of his writing is not important. Perhaps he did, or perhaps he didn't. That can be considered on a case-by-case basis. What is vital is to recognize that the original human authors' intentions is no barrier whatsoever for the divine Author to concurrently embed His intended communication within the text of Scripture with further communicative aims. One of the tenets of a grammatico-historico hermeneutic has to be that the intent of the human authors does not exhaust the literal sense of Scripture since the Holy Spirit binds the Old Testament and the New Testament to God's purpose in Christ.

Second Samuel 5:6–10 is a test case in which Dr. Suk sought to elucidate its *sensus plenior* through the Christocentric redemptive-historical approach. So far the conquest of Jerusalem and the siege of Zion are a recurring theme with definite Christocentric implications of which we have only barely scratched the surface. But apart from the redemptive-historical approach to exemplify and elucidate a *sensus plenior*, the Scriptures are replete with lesser examples. Perhaps some of these are redemptive-historical, but they are not as flashy as King David conquering Zion. In any case, the bronze serpent, Jonah in the whale's belly, Abraham's two wives and two sons, and others are biblical examples of texts obviously requiring a deeper yet single *sensus plenior*.

Consider Galatians 3:24, which says, "Therefore the law was our tutor to bring us to Christ, that we might be justified by faith." Here the apostle Paul, under divine inspiration —or more precisely the divinely inspired biblical text—states that the law had a Christocentric function and intention. By means of the figure of speech called personification, the law is put forth as a pedagogue or teacher. To do what? To lead us to Christ. Why? So that we may be justified. How? Not by the law but by faith.

What Christocentric concord is found in the Word of God!

The whole Bible contains the unfathomable riches of Christ. The Christian interpreter must conclude that it was by the divine inspirer, revealer, and Author of the law that this was so, regardless of the human recipient and author of the law.

This hints at a reality all faithful readers of Scripture must face. The text of Scripture, as a product of God's creation and design, is naturally, in the words of Dr. Mitchell Chase, "a Trinitarian accomplishment. God, by His Spirit, inspires biblical authors to foreshadow and pattern the Son."[25]

In the case of 2 Samuel 5:6–10, however, we've only touched on Zion's typological significance. But if Zion's conquest is typological, we must now come to terms with whether Zion's conqueror, David, is also typological. To conclude so would most certainly not be a fanciful interpretation. In fact, one of

---

25 Originally posted on X, formerly Twitter, by Dr. Mitch Chase (@mitchellchase) on March 8, 2021, at 4:16 p.m.

the major purposes of 2 Samuel was to show how the anointed king of Israel should rule and defend his people. Our passage happens to be a positive portrayal, or snapshot, of what a kingly rule and conquest look like. This ends our excursus, and we continue.

Chapter 5:
Jerusalem and Jesus

3. David Conquered.

David's mindset, words, actions, and ultimate victory are precisely the things the king of Israel had to do. To fall short of any of this would be to fall short of what a king of Israel should be. David's mindset was a commitment to the Lord and His people. Second Samuel 5:3 says that David made a covenant with the tribal leaders of Israel. This mindset led him to go to Jerusalem to pick a fight with the Jebusites. "Live and let live" was not David's mindset. It wasn't "Live and let die" either. David's mindset here was to seek and to destroy the Jebusite trespassers. David's mission is his mindset. David's actions are merely his mindset revealed. His determined hatred for "the blind and the lame" and his devised plan of attack were based on it.

The plan was audacious. It required his mighty men not to scale the walls from the outside but to climb up by way of the water shaft, presumably from within the bulwarks. Difficult? Extremely. Necessary? Absolutely. Audacious? Without a doubt. Likely? The odds were stacked against David and Israel. Verse 7 says, "Nevertheless David took the stronghold of Zion" and renamed it the "City of David."

So I repeat my previous question: Is David, according to this passage, typologically related to Zion's conquest as typological? Zion was the fortress or citadel occupied by the Jebusites in land that didn't belong to them. David rightly conquered it, and it served as the capital of the united kingdom of Israel in the most unlikely circumstances, given Israel's losing streak at the time. Given the subsequent use of the term *Zion* in Scripture as paradigmatic for the people of God or for the place where God is united to His people, it seems textually relevant to link the conquered place with the person who was its conqueror: the anointed king. And just as there is a great gulf between ancient, physical Zion and the Zion whose chief cornerstone is Jesus, the bridge connecting both conquered place and conquering person is the generative text-based category of typology. Yes, David typified Jesus!

But must not types be explicitly identified as such? No, they don't need to be. A type can have either explicit or implicit textual warrant. Dr. Suk's methodology seems correct. If the Bible says that the conquest of Zion is theologically paradigmatic or typological of God's redemption in Christ in purchasing a people, His church, we can conclude that David prefigures or typifies Christ in that conquest. Colossians

1:28 notes, "We proclaim Him, admonishing every person and teaching every person with all wisdom, so that we may present every person complete in Christ" (NASB). But before we proclaim Him, that is Christ, we must labor and strive in His power and in the Spirit's illumination to rightly read Christ's Word. It was He after all who said, "You search the Scriptures, for in them you think you have eternal life; and these are they which testify of Me" (John 5:39).

So now we see the ultimate import of advocating for what is really uncontroversial: a deeper, not dual or quadruple, *sensus plenior* of Scripture. While there may be initial difficulty in drawing out non-obvious meaning beneath the surface of the biblical text, the more you prayerfully train yourself to read correctly, the more you will correctly conclude, by a due use of the ordinary means, that the Christ of Scripture is present in all of Scripture. This is no empty, falsely pious, wishful thinking. The Lord Himself left us with a permanent rebuke for failing to see Him in all of Scripture, as well as our hermeneutical charter in Luke 24:27: "And beginning at Moses and all the Prophets [including 2 Samuel], He expounded to them in all the Scriptures the things concerning Himself."

Why is Christ the warp and woof of Scripture? Simply because He is the warp and woof of all of reality. The order of reality is both Trinitarian and Christological. In fact, for the order of reality to be Christological is for it to be Trinitarian. The Christ of Scripture is the Spirit-anointed king and eternally begotten Son of the Father.

Concluding Thoughts

This leads me to some concluding thoughts. I have five, with the last one expanded for use in sermon prep, Bible study prep, or Sunday school class prep.

Number One

There is both a horizontal and a vertical dimension to perceiving in holy writ the veiled, Christological vistas present throughout the Old Testament. Christian maturity moves from knowing and seeing Christ perhaps only through Messianic prophecies or Christophanies, to figures, types, and shadows. Why? Because as Matt Emerson stated, "The text's ontology demands it, and is the reason Jesus says what he says in Luke 24:27 and Luke 16:31 and John 5:46, among other verses."[26]

> Concurring with his line of thought, Luke Stamps observes,
>
> In the perspective of the New Testament, it's not just that all of the Old Testament is about Christ, all of reality is about him (Colossians 1:15–20) . . . everything in Creation exists from, through, and for the logos. Of course, that is true of the divine economy of redemption recorded in the Old and New Testaments. The whole fabric of this economy is suffused with Christ. The New Testament authors give us the hermeneutical paradigm.

---

26 Originally posted on X, formerly Twitter, by Dr. Matt Emerson (@M_Y_Emerson) on March 12, 2023, at 1:21 p.m.

We have every warrant to see even more types, shadows, and adumbrations of Christ in the Old Testament story.[27]

This is not done in an arbitrary or capricious way, such as with a medieval eisegetical quadriga.

No, it must be done by searching for the internal scriptural bond that emerges when one figural thing, event, or person gives commencement, continuation, or expansion to another thing, event, or person as its maximal expression. Ultimately, the types and shadows are left in the sacred text to be perceived by faithful readers, not by the clever Biblical authors, but by the One who, in the words of Mark Garcia, "is at work in covenant history, throughout creation, providence, and redemption, traversing His own way through history. And history, therefore, and reality [bear] His imprint."[28]

Parenthetically, even as the Lord Jesus commanded His audience to render under Caesar the things that are Caesar's and to God the things that are God's, Part 3 will attempt to render unto God the things of God by shining the light of Scripture on the divine imprint left on reality to rightly interpret the lesser light of nature.

Number Two

Whenever a character in the Bible thinks, speaks, or acts in accordance with the enmity against the serpent, as detailed

---

[27] Originally posted on X, formerly Twitter, by Dr. Luke Stamps (@lukestamps) on March 16, 2023, time unknown.

[28] Mark Garcia, "Jesus Christ and the Lint-Roller? Typology, Figuration, and the Form of the Son," August 6, 2021, in *Greystone Conversations*, produced by Greystone Theological Institute, podcast, 1:03:13, https://podcasts.apple.com/us/podcast/jesus-christ-and-the-lint-roller-typology-figuration/id1518156157?i=1000531176344.

in Genesis 3:15, we must ultimately see the sovereign work of God. God Himself and God alone will put enmity between the woman's redeemed spiritual descendants and the serpent. The conquests of Jerusalem and Zion display precisely that enmity. David, in thought, word, and deed, displayed ultimate loyalty to God as the true king and hatred for his recalcitrant enemies, the Jebusites, for encroaching on God's land and people. The theology of Genesis 3:15 must inform the rest of the Bible, including 2 Samuel 5:6–10, because that enmity always finds expression in redemptive history.

This passage looks backward to Genesis 3:15 as the spiritual source of the spiritual enmity, and through typology it is able to look forward to ultimate Christocentric fulfillment in Jesus. Christ crushes the serpent's head on that cursed fortress known as Golgotha, upon which He shed His blood, and by dying for their sins He purchased, acquired, and secured for Himself a people. This redemptive work is the crimson thread woven throughout Scripture, which, informed by Genesis 3:15, implicitly argues that "all exegesis is ultimately prosopological."[29] That is, we see that the characters in a passage are speaking or acting in a manner that indicates an ongoing spiritual battle that finds future fulfillment in the person and work of Christ the King on His people's behalf. In the case of 2 Samuel 5:6–10, King David speaks from an undivided heart to God just as the anointed king of Israel should be all the time, to carry out His purposes against the serpent's arrogance and defiance. At that particular stage in redemptive history, behind

---

29   Originally posted on X, formerly Twitter, by Dr. Tyler Wittman (@tylerwittman) on March 9, 2021 (since deleted).

the Jebusites was the serpent of old—who is called "the devil" and "Satan"—who deceives the whole world.

NUMBER THREE

The temporal and spiritual stakes cannot be higher. Sin doesn't merely insult or taunt as the Jebusites did. It mortally injures us and separates us from God. Is our hope in kings or princes? As the famous Reformation hymn states,

> *Did we in our own strength confide,*
> *Our striving would be losing;*
> *Were not the right Man on our side,*
> *The man of God's own choosing:*
> *Dost ask who that may be?*
> *Christ Jesus, it is He;*
> *Lord Sabaoth His Name,*
> *From age to age the same,*
> *And he must win the battle.*

This highlights for us the absolute necessity of Christ's office as King. He could have justly excluded us from the confines of His kingdom, but by omnipotent sovereign and efficacious grace the Lord Jesus overcame all obstacles to acquire and redeem a people. And as creation, providence, and redemptive history attest, Christ rules over all things. Christ is our eternal King, who governs us by His Word and Spirit and who defends and preserves us in the enjoyment of that salvation He has purchased for us, as the Heidelberg Catechism says (Question and Answer, 31).

Number Four

This exercise in backwards-engineering Dr. Suk's sermon "The Redemptive Historical Implication of Recapturing Zion" employed typology in the service of Christocentrism. I don't know if Dr. Suk would have agreed with everything I concluded or the means I used to get there, but I tried to privilege the text of Scripture whether it touched upon shadow (type) or substance (anti-type). In the words of Shakespeare put in the mouth of Bessanio concerning the beauty of Portia's portrait and Portia herself, "Yet look how far the substance of my praise doth wrong this shadow in underprizing it, so far this shadow doth limp behind the substance." (The Merchant of Venice, Act 3, Scene 2).

And as I mentioned toward the start, dear reader, maybe you can add more to what I've shared to enhance your understanding of the redemptive-historical implications of recapturing Zion. If so, share with others for the glory of God and to bless your local church. Dig deeper, whether it's a metaphor, a motif, an echo, an organic progression, an expansion, an escalation, a formative influence, a faith tradition in the ancient Israelite community, the analogy of Scripture, a single *sensus plenior*, a paradigm, a prosopological reading, typology, redemptive history—interpreters, at whatever stage of maturity, have to get their hands dirty in handling the text.

The text is pregnant with meaning, and all readers must work smart and hard to arrive at a correct understanding by analyzing and synthesizing what is explicitly and implicitly in the Scriptures. This is what I tried to exemplify in scratching the surface and handling this biblical text. It is simply axiomatic as a Protestant confessional reader of Scripture to be committed to a single *sensus plenior*, as opposed to anything resembling the arbitrary and capricious medieval eisegetical quadriga.

Think of biblical hermeneutics as a large tent. It takes a lot to raise a tent. Regeneration of the reader is the right posture from which you would start, continue, and finish. This spiritual life primes us and reminds us of the Scriptures' divine origin and characteristics. And beyond this, the tools, rope, stakes, and poles required are the previously mentioned strategies consonant with scriptural and theological considerations involved in a right reading. And because of the order of reality itself, Christocentrism in biblical hermeneutics is like the one long tent pole in the middle of a tent. This central, long tent pole makes all the other tent poles, ropes, and pegs worth all the fuss.

Number Five

The rubber meets the road in teaching and preaching 2 Samuel 5:6–10, both pedagogically and homiletically. There's more than one way to skin a cat, and however you decide to skin it, never forget that everyone under your care as a teacher, but especially as a preacher or pastor, is a person who needs to hear and see Jesus. Why? Because the point is not merely to convey facts but also to proclaim the one who is worthy of worship. Who is more worthy than King Jesus?

A sketch of my hybrid homiletical approach is as follows: 2 Samuel 5:6–10 has the theme of David's conquest of Jerusalem and Zion, and the thrust of the passage shows us what was involved in such a kingly conquest. The subject is the kingly conquest of David. The complements, or what can be predicated of that kingly, Davidic conquest, are that it required unity, that it required strategy and tactics, and that it required the Lord of Hosts.

I normally choose to distill the theme and the thrust of a preaching text into a proposition that encompasses both elements completely. This distillation can be called the text's doctrine. For this text it could be this: A king conquers through unity, a plan, and the Lord of Hosts. And so under the aforementioned three heads that delineated what can be predicated of David's kingly conquest according to this passage, I proceeded to develop the exposition by integrating my analysis of the passage accordingly. The resulting homiletical synthesis introduced the passage by reading it and asking what possible reason a believer could have to consider this event so long ago as vital for the Christian life in the here and now.

As the teacher or preacher progresses, some possible reasons can be rejected as to why this passage vitally matters for the believer. These include—to be more like David or to have principles of victorious Christian living. One must clear the road for a more Christocentric and redemptive-historical understanding of this passage. Such an understanding of necessity results in abasing man and exalting God. It argues against man-centeredness and argues for Christ-centeredness.

For example, in the explicit first point, a kingly conquest involves unity between the king and his warriors. We are confronted with a sin problem of inescapable relevance, namely that although the unity was present between David and his mighty men in the conquest of Zion, honesty demands that we confess that we have more in common spiritually speaking with the rebellious Jebusites than we do with David's mighty warriors. We can boast all we want to in our hearts, but all boasting will be brought to naught. Better to "kiss the Son, lest He be angry, and you perish in the way, when His wrath is kindled but a little. Blessed are all those who put their trust in Him" (Psalm 2:12). To trust in God and His precious promises is vital for the Christian here and now.

In the second point, a kingly conquest involves strategic wisdom and tactical cunning. Here the exposition sharpens and the integration takes place between the analysis of the text and the Zion motif by means of the redemptive-historical progression of the Christocentric type and antitype. Once again we are confronted with the problem that sin poses for all of us. Quite simply, if it were up to any of us, we would ruin our situation. There is no shortage of religious ways that seem strategically wise and tactically cunning to rid us of sin, but the end thereof is spiritual destruction (Proverbs 16:25).

This is the ruin we all find ourselves in outside of Christ the King. It is a hopeless and miserable predicament indeed. The good news dawns by means of the eternal decree of God and His meticulous providence in history, which really makes all of history redemptive history. We have, in the text of Scripture from beginning to end, God's strategic wisdom and tactical cunning summed up in the person and work of Christ.

I make no apologies for this Reformed emphasis on the absolute sovereignty, the omnicausal divine decree, and His meticulous providence over all things. What is the alternative?

To put blinders on as I read the Scriptures? Or worse, to put blindfolds on as I preach the Scriptures? Maybe worse yet would be to proclaim from the pulpit the glories of a blind and lame God, no more worthy of worship than the idols of old or the listeners in the audience.

Last, what does 2 Samuel 5:6–10 tell us that a kingly conquest involves?

My answer in point three: A kingly conquest involves the Lord God of Hosts, God incarnate Himself. David's conquest and victory at Zion was temporal. Jerusalem and Zion eventually fell and were trampled underfoot. The Lord Jesus Himself confirmed the finality and apocalyptic destruction of the ancient City of David, but Zion and King David were pictures, or types, of what was to come permanently and spiritually. Truly David has slain his thousands. But the Son of David, the Lord Jesus, has vivified and quickened His tens of thousands. Jesus in His office as King overcame the powers and kingdoms of this world, conquering Zion, even conquering His own people's spiritual death and enmity, to be united to us.

We the church are the true Zion, and we worship the Lord because He has by grace alone converted His Mount Calvary into our Mount Zion. The same eyes of faith that enabled the poor, repentant thief to see Jesus as a king while he bled on the cross can perceive Jesus's kingly shadow cast throughout Old Testament revelation. From this standpoint of faith, the believer can be exhorted and encouraged to be the church militant in the power of the Spirit.

We have a precious promise to cling to as we go forth in spiritual battle: "In that day the Lord will defend the inhabitants of Jerusalem" and that "the one who is feeble among them . . . shall be like David" (Zechariah 12:8).

Such spiritual battle motifs are found throughout the Old Testament and are carried over to the New Testament. A possible allusion to the paradigmatic event of the conquest of Zion can be found in 2 Corinthians 10:3–5: "For though we walk in the flesh, we do not war according to the flesh. For the weapons of our warfare are not carnal but mighty in God for pulling down strongholds, casting down arguments and every high thing that exalts itself against the knowledge of God, bringing every thought into captivity to the obedience of Christ."

PART 3:
THE WORLD

*And in Your majesty ride prosperously
because of truth, humility, and righteousness;
And Your right hand shall teach
You awesome things.
Your arrows are sharp in the heart of the
King's enemies; The peoples fall under You.
Your throne, O God, is forever and ever;
A scepter of righteousness is the scepter of
Your kingdom.*
(Psalm 45:4–6)

Chapter 6:
The Challenge of Christian Education

"I believe in Christianity as I believe that the sun has risen: not only because I see it, but because by it I see everything else."

(C. S. Lewis, *Is Theology Poetry?*)[30]

Introduction

Part Two applied some Christocentric color to Part One's Christocentric tonal underpainting. In this third and final part, we will conclude with further Christocentric colors of the final painting for a finished portrait of Christocentrism as I have reflected on my experience as an elementary school teacher in Christian schools. The continuity and applicability

---

30   C. S. Lewis, "They Asked for a Paper," in *Is Theology Poetry* (London: Geoffrey Bless, 1962), 164.

of the Calvinist account of Christocentrism see no difficulty going from meditation on the Word in the pew on the Lord's Day to meditation on the Word in the world the rest of the days of the week.

In fact, as part of the spiritual warfare that the apostle Paul mentioned in 2 Corinthians 10:3–5, the issues that education introduces to children and touches on are legitimate areas of contested territory. The presuppositions of Christocentrism, which are really just biblical Trinitarian presuppositions, must be wielded in the battle of faith seeking understanding. Even as King David could not countenance containment of the Jebusites, the Calvinist Christian isn't satisfied with integration of faith with reason but subjugation of reason to faith. Conquest, not containment, is the only option for the Calvinist. These issues of faith seeking understanding either reflect a radical dependence on God for ultimate coherence and rationality conformed to Christ the Logos, or they are sound and fury signifying nothing. We believe in order to understand.

Is Christian Education a Luxury or a Necessity?

The education of children is a serious matter. Since it is a fruit of the church's "great salvation," Christian education is a vitally serious matter. To all involved, whether students, parents, administrators, teachers, or the surrounding communities that schools find themselves in, Christian education, rightly conceived and executed, has a unique stamp pointing to the all-encompassing lordship of Christ.

Does it accomplish this by preaching the gospel of salvation? By glorifying missions or evangelizing the lost?

Strictly speaking, no. It does this by self-consciously trying to bring to bear the implications of God's whole revelation to the student in all he or she studies. This certainly does not mean we exclude the message of the good news of God's salvation by grace alone through faith alone in Christ alone. But it does mean that Christian education aims to glorify God by educating students as fully as possible in things foundational, practical, factual, ethical, and systematically true so that they may flourish in whatever their God-given callings may be.

The Christian educator unabashedly embraces and implements a biblical philosophy of education as foundational to dealing with the student and his or her areas of study—inside and out. Therein lies one contrast between public education and Christian education from a Reformed or Calvinistic perspective. The means and ends of the respective educational philosophies carried out in public and private Christian schools are strikingly two poles apart. And necessarily so—acutely so for the Calvinist!

Calvinists are handicapped by, among other things, the strange visual impairment of recognizing that the truth of the Bible applies to every person on this earth, to every subject to be studied, and to every aspect of life! From a Reformed perspective, a fully-orbed Christian philosophy of education makes all the difference in education because it sets forth what must be taught, how it must be taught, why it must be taught, what must be learned, how it must be learned, why it must be learned, and finally what must be lived, how it must be lived, and why it must be lived. This all-encompassing Reformed philosophy is derived from biblical truths and principles and applies at least as much to the adults as to the children bestowed in our care.

Conversions, decisions of faith, and discipleship will arise. Barriers to such things will be taken down as much as possible. Christian educators should view cooperation with local churches as indispensable in this regard. But again, to put it another way, Christian education at its best is designed to be the outworking of a reflective Christian faith in all educational areas for the glory of God and the good of the student. After all, the God of the gospel leaves nothing in His world and our lives unturned.

What then is meant by saying Christian education offers a unique mark pointing to the all-encompassing lordship of Christ? What does it mean for a Christian educator to self-consciously bring to bear the implications of God's whole revelation in all areas of study? Although God has been marked "absent" in public education for years, private Christian K-12 schools too often have low expectations for God's attendance in their classrooms. Is God really "in attendance" in Christian schools? It matters. How could the axiom of Christianity not make all the difference in the world for education? The Bible alone is the Word of God!

This royal presupposition is our life's blood, our lungs' air, our only sustenance, our only solid ground. The remainder of this final part will attempt to take a panoramic snapshot of Christian education in answering these and other related questions.

Even if the Christian teacher does not presently share this Reformed enthusiasm for and vision of Christian education, I hope my efforts will enhance his or her present working knowledge of the contours of a Christian worldview. I hope that Christian educators, at whatever level they teach or in whatever system they teach, will be encouraged, inspired, and have their faith strengthened in their reflective process. Offered heartily to all Christian teachers is a way to apply the fortunes of Christianity in the classroom as a Reformed heart sees it.

The Challenge Stated

Christian schools face such a grave responsibility to families, local churches, their communities, and the body of Christ that they should be ever mindful of God's approving or disapproving eye upon the service they render. Does our service reflect this mindfulness? If not, what does that say about us? What does it portray about our beliefs?

Christian theology makes a valuable contribution to educational theory and practice. Christian schools and public schools inevitably impact individual lives and the culture at large. Therefore, Christian educators should seriously consider how they carry out their calling and consider how the fortunes of a Christian worldview can enrich their understanding and appreciation of the teaching profession.

As though this self-reflective process weren't challenging enough with all the busyness of our duties in the school year, another fundamental challenge touches on everything we do as teachers in Christian schools. It should be resolved before the school year starts and certainly before a teacher steps into the classroom, but too often it isn't. The challenge is both heavenly and earthly. It is at once existential, epistemological, and everyday.

The greatest challenge of Christian education is recognizing the unifying principle that not only sustains us through the vicissitudes of our task but also gives rich and lasting meaning in the joys we take part in as well. Reformed theology provides that unifying principle because it invests all of life with a radically scriptural "God significance." God undoubtedly looks upon us approvingly when we seek His glory in all areas of education by recognizing His significance in those areas. It should be no surprise that God has an "opinion" on educational matters.

In ancient biblical times, education was familial in most cultures. God's people were mandated to teach their children His statutes, commandments, and mighty acts and judgments. They were commanded to fear God and to serve Him in love and gratitude for His mercy and grace upon them. Since God was their Creator, Redeemer, and deliverer from bondage, He expected the Israelites to devote themselves wholeheartedly to their covenant God. Commitment and allegiance to Him alone were their ultimate responsibility. He commanded Israelites to shun false gods and do what was right and good in the sight of the Lord.

By contrast, the inhabitants of the Promised Land did not serve the true God. Their education undoubtedly prepared their children and youth for productive, independent adult life in some trade, skill, or profession. However, their lives were lived in the context of the great sin of recalcitrant unbelief in the one true God. Their devotion was to falsehood, and their activities, "religious" or otherwise, were inextricably connected to their ultimate commitment to false gods. It is no wonder that God regarded not only their religious practices (Proverbs 15:8) but also their mundane activities (Proverbs 21:4) as different faces of sin.

Despite appearances, the crown rights of God reach everyone and everything. In light of this, the Israelites' mission was understandable: to drive out the inhabitants of Canaan because there could be no integration between a people of truth and a people of falsehood. There could be no neutrality between the two people groups in the issues of life, especially concerning education, since education is the medium through which truth or error is transmitted on life's issues.

We, however, are not in ancient biblical times or lands. Ours is an increasingly crumbling post-Christian, relativistic era. Although our mandate is not the conquest of Canaan, are we not called to be a peculiar people unto our covenant God? If we teachers are not mindful of what God approves of or disapproves of in matters of education, how can the service we render in our Lord's name and under the banner of Christian education be authentic? That would be like an Israelite fashioning an idol and devoting himself to it in thought, word, and deed as a Canaanite might do and considering it no big deal!

What, then, is special about the service we render amid our shattered and decaying culture?

Many things make Christian education unique. As Reformed thought sees it, and as my focus will be, the applicability of God's Word to all areas of knowledge is paramount and a singular feature of Christian education. My focus will be to examine the applicability of God's Word to a couple of areas of God's world, although I can only scratch the surface.

The Educational Antithesis

Christian schools are not in the business of producing citizens for the benefit of the state. We aren't teaching to prepare students for a career, to ensure a robust national or world economy, or even to sloganeer the chants of human rights. The values we hold or desire to pass on are not of personal peace and affluence. Nor does it involve the ever-changing "common good." The purposes for which Christian education exists and the reasons we teach in such schools transcend this world (but without ignoring it, of course).

A four-word phrase summarizes the purpose of Christian education and why we work as teachers in a Christian school: *the glory of God.*

The glory of God should find full expression in all we believe and, specifically, in all we teach. This emphasis is all-encompassing, for as Reformed theology maintains, the whole world—things visible and invisible—is "the theater of God's glory." With the Bible as our guide, and through the discerning theological eyes of faith, we seek to discover how and why God and His Word apply to everything from visible things, like the manifold wonders of creation and providence in history, to invisible things, like the many facets of divine truth in places we would never have thought to look for them (much less find them) such as in mathematics.

This uniquely Christian emphasis highlights the Christian basis for unity in truth and life for the student.

The only question is, *Will Christian schools take the time and expend the effort to discover what is already present within the subjects we teach, namely, a radically scriptural God significance?*

Let the believer who limits God to a select realm of knowledge bear the burden of demonstrating for all, including God, that He is bound to only those territories of truth! We might as well say that God is bound to the land of Palestine. This is dishonoring to God, His truth, and His all-encompassing lordship. The immensity of God by His essential nature admits no rivals when it comes to grounding truth in all areas, not just the Bible and ethics. He who cannot be localized, limited, or lessened accounts for all reality because He is fullness of being Himself. He exists in everything we see or do not see, feel or do not feel. As the apostle Paul argued publicly to the philosophers at Mars Hill, "In Him we live and move and have our being" (Acts 17:28). Paul was no innovator. The prophet Jeremiah records God's rhetorical question thus:

> "*Am* I a God near at hand," says the Lord,
> "And not a God afar off?
> Can anyone hide himself in secret places,
> So I shall not see him?" says the Lord;
> "Do I not fill heaven and earth?" says the Lord. (Jeremiah 23:23–24)

As Reformed philosopher Cornelius Plantinga writes, a distinctly Christian education doesn't offer an "education-as-usual with Bible classes tacked on, or education-as-usual with prayers before class. . . . No, a solidly built Christian [school] will rise from its faith in Jesus Christ and then explore the height and depth, the length and breadth of what it means to build on this faith . . . for a lifetime of learning and work within the kingdom of God." Quoting approvingly from the Puritan founders of Harvard, Plantinga writes that education and learning "will lay Christ in the bottome (sic)."[31] If this approach is sound, this Christocentric "bottom" or foundation is applicable not only to university or doctoral-level academia but also to elementary and secondary education.

The applicability of the truth of Christ's Word must be seen at the core of Christian education and flow throughout everything we teach by lesson and life. A thin veneer of Christianity will not do. A thin veneer of Christianity over education is nothing more than education-as-usual with Bible and prayer tacked on. Christian teachers should not put limits on God by thinking that God applies only to the Bible or ethics but not to other subjects.

Christian teachers at their best carry out their duties in worshipful awe of God's presence in every realm of knowledge. This divine immensity invests our vocation with meaning. This is what unifies God's truth with our lives. We are co-laborers with Him, standing before students and proclaiming, "This subject matter is His!" Non-Christian thought can't even begin to approximate what we have in God's truth and the foundation it provides for unity with all of life.

GODLESS EDUCATION

I will flesh out how a Christian view of education is unique and distinctive by contrasting it with a non-Christian educator's words on education. Although Kristen Olsen Lanier is not

---

31 Cornelius Plantinga, *Engaging God's World: A Christian Vision of Faith, Learning, and Living* (Grand Rapids, MI: Eerdmans, 2002), xiv.

operating from a Christian faith reference point, I want to affirm her motivation to tackle deep issues in education as commendable. However, her words vividly illustrate with great force to Christian educators the contrast between what passes for the outcomes of education for non-believers and believers.

In an article titled "Food for Thought" she writes, "Good, thoughtful work in schools—work that occurs too infrequently in the classroom as evidenced by the weekly packets sent home to me as a parent—helps individuals [look] . . . at real, profound questions of human existence and assumes that children can wrestle with these issues—that their minds will be enlarged and made muscular by such struggles."[32] These words would be commendable if their meaning were invested with biblically informed assumptions, including a Christian view of creation and human nature created in God's image. As it is, they are not, and their deficiency comes out all the more clearly. Lanier builds her commentary on good, thoughtful schoolwork around one issue: "the complex problem of holding two remarkably contradictory ideas in your mind at once, without resolving the dilemma on either side." This, it would seem, is a virtue to Lanier.

She charmingly illustrates the dilemma with an anecdote about buying a live mouse to feed to her son's new pet snake. What an uncomfortable decision! Parents can especially sympathize with her situation. In considering the issue at the pet store with her children, Lanier mused that while it is "good and important to care about individual mice, to think that the

---

32 Kirsten Olsen Lanier, "Food for Thought," *Teacher Magazine*, August/September 2000, 69.

life of a mouse is important," it is also good for them to purchase a live mouse to use as food for their snake. Apparently, one good canceled out the other good. This contradiction was tolerated because of the "certain knowledge that things must eat each other to live." Little comfort for the mouse!

The real issue is not animal survival but the value she places on holding to contradictions. She calls holding to two mutually exclusive thoughts "[holding] on to both the snake and the mouse."

Charming—but wrong.

Her solution to have children's minds strengthened by profound questions of human existence disappoints. It must be because it is not grounded in God's Word. Lanier prescribes that children (and by implication all people) resolve life's profound questions through a process of "holding two contradictory ideas at once." Instead of enlarging minds, it impoverishes them and makes education the presentation and the propagation of the irrational.

But all this is really illustrative of the intellectual struggle, the educational antithesis, between Christianity and all non-Christian thought. Anything can constitute a valid perspective if the revelation from God is not the foundation of knowledge. Since present non-Christian thought leaves little room for absolute truth (except for the "truth" that there is no absolute truth!), it is perfectly acceptable to hold on to two mutually exclusive positions. One position is as good as the other. From a non-Christian standpoint, anything goes intellectually (and for that matter, morally)—*even contradictions.*

This is definitely not commendable for Christian educators, but from Lanier's perspective it is worth lamenting that more schools don't have "sufficient confidence in children that they will ultimately understand and be enriched by such messiness." Such "Food for Thought" can only malnourish both children and teachers. At best, from a Christian perspective her view is naive. It expects rational beings to see the profound issues of life through the lens of the irrational—contradictions—and to live with them.

Ironically, what Lanier advocates is already the pervasive and systematic practice in our schools. What she laments as infrequently taking place happens all too often. That's part of our society's problem!

Doesn't experience, especially recent experience, show that children have wrestled passionately with profound questions of human existence? But their education from K to 12 has guided them to embrace the lack of objective unity between what they have been taught and what their community expects from them. The most obvious general example is the ethical relativism rampant in the educational establishment. These concepts, whether caught or taught, often encroach on parents' rights to instill in their children moral standards differing from those of the state. Take for example Christian parents' instruction regarding gender identity as they believe it to be found in the Scriptures and how some states allow for schools to influence the moral formation of young children to embrace non-binary sexuality or other views inconsistent with or contrary to traditional Christian views and hide it from their parents. The issue of the value of life is also in the forefront of many young people's lives. It is not at all uncommon in some places for elementary school children to carry firearms wherever they go. I have seen this happen in eighth-grade graduations or school sporting events. This practice has developed for several reasons, and we cannot exclude the moral relativism expressed in public education.

Public school teachers avowedly aim for human progress, but they expect it ultimately to be reached by the moral relativism that is guaranteed by the rejection of God's book of nature and book of Scripture. And this shows that the decisive battle has already taken place in state-sponsored education. Everything that happens afterward is simply the mopping-up job. Tragically, some of what gets mopped up nowadays is actual blood in the violence and death that take place in or near schools. Gordon H. Clark asks,

> How does God judge the school system which says to him, "O God, we neither deny nor assert thy existence; and God, we neither obey nor disobey thy commands; we are strictly neutral"? Let no one fail to see the point: the school system that ignores God teaches its pupils to ignore God; and this is not neutrality. It is the worst form of antagonism, for it judges God to be unimportant and irrelevant in human affairs. This is atheism.[33]

Experience shows that the best that non-Christian instructors can offer is an education that yields only candy-

---

[33] Gordon H. Clark, *A Christian Philosophy of Education*, 3rd ed. (Jefferson, MD: The Trinity Foundation, 2000), 55.

coated despair on the one hand or candy-coated delusions on the other.

I don't mean to suggest that only Christian learners develop academic competencies. That would be ridiculous. I am suggesting that only through a Christian worldview can teachers and students make sense of it all. Only a distinctly Christian education yields a rational foundation for all truth and its unity with their lives.

Chapter 7:
The Antithesis Confirmed: Science and History

Where does the rubber meet the road for Christian education?

Briefly, consider both science and history since their content somewhat overlaps. (Keep in mind that no matter how much we may wish to avoid it, ethics rears its head in any such discussion as well.) These disciplines ask and attempt to answer the profound questions "What is there?" and "Where is it all going?" respectively.

Science

A child will ask, "What is life and where did it come from?" The education-as-usual response is that through incredible naturalistic processes, *first*, the conditions and elements necessary to form a living thing just fortuitously came about; *second*, many of those ingredients just got together and blindly synergized in the most hostile of environmental conditions; and *third*, they've been effervescing and, despite the degenerative effects of random mutations, have just been growing increasingly complex and adaptive ever since, so much so that even our very thoughts are the products of this naturalistic, evolutionary process.

Our bodies, our minds, and even the deliverances of our minds are geared toward surviving and passing on our genes. Survival takes primacy. Since everything about us is geared toward surviving, from physical traits to our faculties and their deliverances, truth is not important in any area. This two piece combo of naturalism and evolution immediately faces a tiny difficulty as a consequence: it is impossible to maintain it rationally! After all, you were evolved to believe it![34]

This insurmountable problem leaves the believer in naturalistic evolution with no basis for confidence that his naturalistic point of view is in fact rational. It is positively self-defeating. No less a proponent of this naturalistic perspective than Charles Darwin himself had doubts. He would not be allowed to express them if he taught in a public high school today.

We can therefore discern a fundamental contrast between the education-as-usual answer to biological science and what ought to be taught to students in Christian education settings. Furthermore, notice that non-Christian education is opposed to Christian education because of Christian education's primary concern for truth in every sphere of knowledge, including science.

---

34   Alvin Plantinga, *Where The Conflict Really Lies: Science, Religion, & Naturalism* (New York, NY: Oxford University Press, 2011), xiv.

We seek to equip students with the very tools that bring to bear Christ, who is the way, the truth, and the life of all their studies. Education in the truth demands exclusive and all-encompassing allegiance to the only source of truth in all areas of knowledge. There can be no neutrality.

The dark side of the naturalistic equation is that what ought to be, morals, cannot be objectively derived from what is—the observable world. Children who accept what they have soaked in throughout their education may and often do logically reach a conclusion of despair and are easily identifiable in schools nationwide. They were not given an adequate moral compass to differentiate between good and evil. To borrow imagery from Kirsten Lanier, perhaps the good is the mouse and the evil is the snake—or vice-versa. Again, this is not to suggest that only Christian students can develop morally or that all moral questions are unambiguous or absolute. However, the naturalism promoted in public education not only has moral ambiguity in the application of ethics but also ambiguity in accounting for the basis or foundation of morality itself. This is a price tag too high to pay both rationally and practically for a believer in Jesus, who is the way, the truth, and the life.

Without God and His Word, we must hold on to the snake and the mouse. One is as valid as the other in a naturalistic worldview. When students realize this, they ask themselves, "What's the difference? Why does my life matter? Why do my studies matter? Is wrestling with these questions even worth it?" At least they are honest enough to ask the tough questions. Not receiving coherent answers and not knowing what to think of the significance of their lives, they embrace despair.

History

Students soak in such metaphysical naturalism through the years as they are simultaneously guided in their studies of history to conclude that since history has no meaningful beginning, it does not have a meaningful continuation or culmination other than what individuals or political entities construct for themselves. (If we turn to science for knowledge of a cosmic culmination, it assures us only of the ultimate heat destruction of the universe—too long ahead of us to matter.)

Naturalistic views of history tell us that our world is all there is and no explanation from above is allowed, much less warranted. Yet students are also taught to make evaluations of persons and events. This person is good and that event is evil. Of course, different individuals and societies will reach opposite conclusions. But what other basis than human convention does our educational system provide for students?

As the students get older, they reason that even as humans generally have no objective purpose beyond this world, individuals in particular may construct reality for themselves. This very conclusion is the desired learning outcome in the non-Christian educational setting. It is often held up to encourage students to "make the world a better place."

Many students are convinced that this is the best road to take. Instead of despair, the student is encouraged to "make the world a better place" and chooses hope for the future, hope that humanity will work to make the world a better place tomorrow.

But here are unasked questions these students aren't equipped to answer: Who decides what is "better"? On what basis is one path "better" than another? Do votes or numbers determine what is good, evil, false, or true? The Lord Jesus Christ came proclaiming glad tidings and He was killed for it. To His society they were obviously not glad tidings, and His proclamation was found worthy of a cruel and profane death.

Upon what objective basis can the student (and by implication, the teacher who advocates an optimistic outlook for humanity's future) be justifiably optimistic that his or her ideals, however they were arrived at, (1) should be the ones that others should strive for and (2) will triumph in the future? Even if they do triumph to any degree, how long will they last—and is it worth it?

These questions, and the apparently intractable propensity among humans to destroy things and kill each other, make optimists uncomfortable. At least science relegates our ultimate doom far off into the future. History testifies that as humanity increases in the technical knowledge derived from education-as-usual, we are that much more destructive of our world and each other in the here and now! Such teachers and students must ignore the tough questions to retain their optimism and hence the delusion.

THE WHOLE COUNSEL OF CHRIST

Praise be to God that we don't have an irrational, fragmented worldview! Glory to God that of Him and through Him and to Him are all things! Thank God that He has given us His Word, without which we would be in despair or delusion.

The Christian educator rejoices over the fact that, as Reformed philosopher Gordon H. Clark stated, "Christianity is a comprehensive view of all things: it takes the world, both material and spiritual, to be an ordered system," each part deriving its significance from the whole.[35]

Christianity therefore encompasses as much as Christ's lordship—everything! What ancient pagan poets and philosophers groped in the dark to find was in the fullness of time revealed to be clearly and properly found in Christ, the image of the invisible God in whom we all live and move and have our being.

Dutch Reformed theologian Herman Bavinck identifies a Trinitarian motif that can be adapted by Christian educators to locate a subject's relation to God and thus a view of how God's truth is the foundation for all truth. Any teacher can use his short synopsis of the faith and seek to discover the big scriptural Trinitarian God picture provided by our subjects. He summarized, "The essence of the Christian religion is this, that the creation of the Father, devastated by sin, is restored in the death of the Son of God, and re-created by the Holy Spirit into a kingdom of God."[36]

Let me explain, however superficially, how this can provide for unity in truth and life in the educational process of dealing with the profound questions of human existence.

As we have seen, science and its presupposed methodological naturalism sees all observable and non-observable reality to exist by unguided, blind chance. By

---

[35] Gordon H. Clark, *A Christian View of Man and Things* (Jefferson, MD: The Trinity Foundation, 1991), 25.
[36] Herman Bavinck, *In the Beginning: Foundations of Creation Theology* (Grand Rapids, MI: Baker Books, 1999), 16, as quoted from his *Gereformeerde Dogmatiek*, vol. I, 4th ed. (Kampen: Kok, 1928), 89.

contrast, the Christian's starting point takes Scripture as a special revelation from God and presupposes that the world is uninterpretable by naturalistic lenses. The world and all facets of reality aren't brute facts, the results of unguided, blind chance. Things visible and invisible must be mediated and subjugated by the Christ of Scripture who is the Logos. A Christless book of nature can only supplant Christ if it tries to supplement Christ's book of Scripture. For the Reformed believer, God's book of Scripture must not only complement His book of nature but also breathe the breath of life into it in order for it to paint an adequate picture of the Christocentric and trinitarian order of reality.

Creation is complex and has been so from the start by the inseparable operations of God's design. It is radically informational, despite the degenerative effects of the fall, and continues to "groan" in anticipation of its restoration brought about by Christ's finished work applied by the Holy Spirit. The world and all therein are what we would expect, given the biblical creation account. We may see through a glass darkly in what we study in the sciences, but the alternative to doing science in a Christian way is doing science irrationally, as irrational as having confidence in blind and lame idols or as countenancing contradictions without resolving them.

Similarly, the history of the world is providentially guided by God to glorify Him in the formation and advancement of His kingdom, of which the church plays a central role. Neither tyrants nor evil have the last word in the affairs of men. And this was decisively demonstrated and portrayed by the determinate counsel of God in the crucifixion of Christ. It reversed the fall of man and achieved the death of death itself.

We may not have an exhaustively detailed account of all of history, but the only alternative to doing history in a Christian way ultimately results in either candy coated delusion or candy coated despair. We have Scripture to provide us with the major contours of history and their direct relationship to us. History is hinged on the irrefutable resurrection of Jesus on the repentant sinner's behalf.

All scientists and historians, whether believers or not, will one day bow their knees and confess with their tongues that Jesus Christ is Lord.

Chapter 8:
The Antithesis Confirmed: Language and Math

Language

Children ask other profound questions of human existence that I would like to bring to your attention. To begin with, seventh-grader Sarah may ask, "You know . . . like . . . where did language and like all that come from?"

Of course, we won't drop the ball and answer that language is the evolved grunts and growls of evolved primates that helped them survive in their environments. Language is the gift of God to man, given to communicate among ourselves and most importantly given for us to have a true knowledge of Him. Therefore, a Christian teacher can appropriately start off the school year by telling Sarah and the rest of the students that learning how to express oneself well is a spiritual exercise. From a biblical standpoint, communication has great dignity. The pertinent Trinitarian consideration is this: even as the persons of the Trinity have spoken to each other from eternity and from the beginning to us through intelligible utterances, so do we.

It pleased God to reveal His Word to us through a book with different genres, with poetry, prose, narrative, with all kinds of literary devices to communicate a knowledge of Himself and His works. Respect for language, for the only adequate vehicle for intelligible thought, points to a reverence for God, since language comes from Him. With this in mind, we guide and encourage our students to learn the parts of speech, to learn proper grammar, to learn the mechanics of language, to read between the lines, to express intellectual creativity, and to do all this to display God's magnificence to each other's edification and for the advancement of His kingdom.

Now this doesn't mean that all our students without exception will become Christian Homers, Shakespeares, Poes, Faulkners, Hemingways, or Maya Angelous because of their thoughtful efforts. It doesn't even mean that our students will always write a clear message to put on the refrigerator, for that matter. But it does mean that they have been given a basis to appreciate the true worth of their studies. It is a worth that only Christianity invests in their education. Some will use their academic competencies in the area of language for downright rebellious, anger-driven, anti-Christian purposes and be successful and influential at it. In that case, we shouldn't lose heart but should humbly submit before God's sovereign will, knowing that "Surely the wrath of man shall praise [God]" (Psalm 76:10). We place our confidence in God alone because His wise, holy, and sovereign purposes can't be thwarted. He is in control.

Whatever the outcome, teachers have said that language along with other areas of study belong to King Jesus, and we have resolved to do nothing less than to fight for His crown rights here and across the curriculum one day at a time, one lesson at a time, and one student at a time.

MATH

What about mathematics? Surely mathematics can't be Christian, can it? Math is neutral, isn't it?

Consider the nature of mathematics for a moment. Take it slowly. Bring your presuppositions forward. Your Christian presuppositions. Ready? I can't hope to go too deeply into it. God hasn't given me the ability. Perhaps He has given you the knowledge to dig deeper. If so, share your thoughts with me and others for His glory!

But here is another one of those profound questions of human existence: Rambunctious fourth-grader Johnny is learning his multiplication tables and asks his teacher, "Yo, Mrs. V.—like, where do math and numbers and all that come from anyway?"

How should we explain or account for mathematical truth?

If we go to the local bookstore, library, or university for answers, we'll encounter two general answers that flow from approaches antagonistic toward Christianity.[37] One answer to the problem of where math comes from is that math is

---

[37] Russell W. Howell and W. James Bradley, eds., *Mathematics in a Postmodern Age: A Christian Perspective* (Grand Rapids, MI: Eerdmans, 2001), 20.

the function of brains. Their type of thinking depends on research, experiments, and theories about consciousness from which inferences are drawn to show that math is literally all in our heads. Let's call this "the materialist math answer." The other answer to the problem of where math comes from is that math *just is*. Their type of thinking rejects most research and experiments as irrelevant and instead is more analytic about theories and about defining its terms but fails to ground mathematics on anything transcendent. Let's call this "the mere metaphysical math answer." The former answer is presumptuously wrong while the latter is humbly mistaken. Both approach the dilemma posed by math from non-Christian presuppositions.

Any way you look at it, math is a shared reality. After all, Christians and non-Christians alike deposit and withdraw funds from their bank accounts. The difference is, as Reformed apologist Cornelius Van Til wryly stated in his classes, that while non-believers can count, they cannot account for counting.[38] The Christian worldview alone provides a rational ground for the properties that everyone attributes, knowingly or unknowingly, to mathematical truth.

THE MATERIALIST ANSWER

Christian teachers can deal with the materialist math answer in two ways. First, we must reject the basic materialist contention that mathematical thinking must be construed as activity in brains instead of the universal, non-physical

---

[38] Timothy Paul Jones, "Apologetics: Did Cornelius Van Til Really Teach that Non-Christians Know Nothing?", *Apologetics* (blog), February 11, 2020, www.timothypauljones.com/apologetics-what-critics-of-cornelius-van-til-get-wrong/.

activity in non-physical minds. Second, we may reveal the major embarrassment in such a materialist math answer.

The materialist math answer will grant that mathematical truth is mental but will define *mind* to mean nothing more than "brain." Toes wiggle, tongues taste, glands secrete, and brains think mathematics. The materialist reduces any kind of thinking to chemical or physiological activity in our physical, material heads.

Right away, though, the question arises as to how they can justify calling chemical, physical, or neurological activity either true or false. In redefining *mind* to mean "brain," materialists have denied themselves any possibility of valid argumentation to justify an acceptance of their position. Why? Because physical motions in our heads cannot produce what the physical motions in someone else's head would have any obligation to accept as the rationality of a valid argument.

We all agree that mathematical truth is mental, but only propositions (which are non-material) can be the objects of knowledge in minds (which are also non-material). Physiological activity in a brain is just a bodily change. No matter how much we observe and experiment with the brain, we cannot derive propositions to construct an argument from it that warrants our acceptance of the materialist math answer. Materialists, in redefining *mind* to mean "brain," have done Christians a favor in demolishing their own position.

To reduce any mathematical truth as elementary as $2 \times 2 = 4$ to physical motions in the brain erects other insurmountable problems: (1) no one person can have the same mathematical thought twice since any thought we have is a "fleeting event numerically distinct from every other"[39] due to its physiological nature; (2) no two persons can share the same mathematical thought at all because the juices that flow in one brain are different from the juices that flow in another brain; (3) as a consequence of reducing mathematical truth in such a materialist fashion, no one could repeat the same thought twice (making memory impossible), nor could one receive another's identical thought (making communication impossible).

We may end our rejection of the materialist math answer by revealing its major embarrassment. Since Christians would clearly have to be committed to a view of mathematical truth that transcends the material world and the materialist would object, we can simply reply that based on his own terms, "his denial [of our position] must be conceived to exist in his own mind only; and since it has not registered in any other mind, it does not occur to us to refute it."[40]

What, then, can we tell Johnny about math? We can tell him and the rest of the class that mathematical truth exists universally, it exists mentally and not materially, and that our minds are judged by math. In the classroom, teachers declare only whether students have reasoned their way through a problem correctly or not. We don't manufacture its truth. We aren't the basis of mathematics. Students sometimes even catch our mistakes at the board (chalkboard, whiteboard, or Smart Board) and let us know that we haven't reasoned our way through a problem either. I hate when that happens!

---

[39] Gordon H. Clark, *A Christian View of Man and Things* (Jefferson, MD: The Trinity Foundation, 1991), 320.

[40] Clark, *A Christian View*, 320.

Some years ago the lives of Enron and Arthur Anderson employees were being affected by omnipresent and unwavering mathematical truth. (Sadly, one of those people, embracing despair, committed suicide because he wanted to avoid being held accountable for his part in violating mathematical absolutes.)

It is also apparent that mathematical truths defy matter and space because such truths can be present in more than one place. We can also say that mathematical truths defy time because such truths never began nor will ever end. 2 x 2 = 4 was true before any of us was conceived and will be true after we're long gone.

This is just for starters.

THE METAPHYSICAL ANSWER

Because of the difficulties of the materialist math answer, some offer "the mere metaphysical math answer." This answer recognizes certain mathematical properties and the inadequate account for them by materialists. Proponents of "the mere metaphysical math answer" rightly define the term *mind* to mean something non-physical so as to preserve a consistent basis for memory and communication. (Remember that one form of communication is sharing a valid argument.) These folks stand in awe of the order, beauty, and universality of math and like to talk of the mystery of it all.

Of course, math neither begins nor ends. Of course, math defies matter, space, and time—but why?

Given the qualities of mathematical truth already mentioned, what else does mathematical truth imply? We can also say that math is unchanging. We can also say that math is superior to any one of our minds and to all human minds. Proponents of "the mere metaphysical math answer" engage in pedantic discussions of terms and definitions but are hard-pressed to account for mathematics' immutability or superiority to the human mind. They rightly humble themselves in light of their finiteness. They wrongly humble themselves before mathematics.

They offer no basis for why math is just out there, but they do admit that the foundation for math cannot be something limited or temporary. The foundations of math have to resemble the properties of math. Rejecting the Bible as God's Word from the start, proponents of "the mere metaphysical math answer" offer a solution incompatible with allegiance to the all-encompassing lordship of Christ. Although the Christian parent or Christian teacher might think so, the Lord of Heaven and Earth doesn't consider mathematical truth neutral territory.

As I see it, our Lord looks upon mathematics as He does everything else and declares, "This is mine!"

Christians can account for mathematics on the basis of the biblical triune depiction of God. If truth exists, including mathematical truth, its basis is God, whose attributes are reflected in the properties of math. Is mathematical truth unchanging? God is unchanging. Is mathematical truth eternal? Only because God is. Does mathematical truth defy matter, space, time? So does God, because He is Spirit, and the fullness of His being is maximally immense and supreme. Is mathematical truth an object of thought in non-physical minds and yet superior to human minds? Well, God's mind is omniscient, knowing all truths. Do we stand in judgment of mathematical truth? Not any more than we stand in judgment of God.

Math is not just out there as a mysterious curiosity of the universe. Math pervades all of our lives because God pervades all of our lives. A Christian's reflection upon math positions him to stand in awe not of it but of the tri-personal God of the Scriptures (see Psalm 139:17–18). Since mathematical truth manifests certain properties consonant with the attributes of God as revealed in His Word of truth, the basis and ground for mathematical truth are that God Himself is truth (Deuteronomy 32:4; John 14:6; John 16:13—a Trinitarian emphasis on God as truth).

We can lead students through these considerations, and they will respond with their own examples of mathematical truths taught by God. I've experienced it during my years as a teacher and a parent.

The upshot of these Christian mathematical musings is that when any of us learn math, we also get to know something of God's nature, because mathematical truths are among "the eternal thoughts of God. And insofar as man knows anything, he is in contact with God's mind. Since, further, God's mind is God, we may legitimately borrow the figurative language, if not the precise meaning, of the mystics and say, we have a vision of God."[41]

Glory be to the triune God of Scripture!

---

[41] Clark, *A Christian View*, 321.

The Role of Education in God's Plan

Christian education in whatever manner it is implemented and executed (home school, private school, classical school, co-op, or at the kitchen table in addition to public school education) is a worthwhile necessity that displays a unique spiritual antithesis to the run-of-the-mill secular education being offered for the so-called common good.

But God gave children to their parents, not the government or a village. We do, however, have the freedom and responsibility to carry out directly or by delegation the education of our children for their good and for the glory of God. How do we accomplish this?

By seeing Christ, the Christ of Scripture, in all of education!

It seems to me that sharing about scratching the surface of the applicability of God's truth to profound issues of human existence is necessary if we want to develop in our students a Christ-honoring biblical worldview. Teachers must bounce ideas off each other. We must collaborate. We must hold each other accountable. In his *Basic Concepts in Christian Pedagogy*, Jan Waterink writes, "It is the task of the elementary school to do everything in its power to have [a] comprehensive view of the revelation of God . . . developed in the child by the time he is approximately twelve to fourteen years of age,"[42] and we can only guide the child's development in this academic and lifelong process by mediating and subjugating our knowledge of the world to the truth of God, because the whole world is God's, and God's truth is all truth.

---

42 Jan Waterink, *Basic Concepts in Christian Pedagogy* (Grand Rapids, MI: Eerdmans, 1954), 129.

God is not neutral, after all, about anything that sets itself up to be believed as truth. Education has a non-neutral character. One is either promoting faith in God and His truth, as the Israelites were, or working against it, as the Jebusites were. But our task is compounded if the teacher himself or herself fails to realize the implications of a Christian worldview for education. That's why we must sharpen each other as iron sharpens iron. No one knows it all.

For far too long God has been marked "absent" in education. This should not be so in Christian schools or in Christian homes. The presupposition that God is and that He has revealed Himself in the Scriptures of the Old and New covenant makes all the difference in the world. All educational experiences and curriculum, therefore, ought to be contextualized on this biblical basis. Reformed thought sees this as the beginning of wisdom for a genuinely Christian education.

Thus, a genuine philosophy of Christian education, echoing Reformed theology, provides a strong framework within which all involved in the educational process can make wise, Biblically informed choices about how to think and act. Thinking and acting biblically are the means of satisfying the King's will, flourishing as humans, subduing the earth, and bringing every thought captive to the obedience of Christ in whatever students study and do. Seeing Christ in all of education establishes that God's truth is all truth and should be imparted God's way. A biblical philosophy of Christian education, echoing Reformed theology, demands that precept and practice harmonize to the glory of God and for the good of the students. In so doing, the benefits will be palpable to the community, the church, and the world.

Chapter 9:
Concluding Remarks

The fortunes of a Christocentric worldview are many. They flow from the trinitarian throne of grace to our world. We can know this by attending to the voice of the Word of God Incarnate by means of the Word of God inscripturated. From Christ's voice in His Word, we can tease out the myriad applications and implications for His world. The unity in truth with our lives is grounded in the triune purpose of God in Christ to be all in all. Only then can the saved see and savor the continuity between a Christocentric interpretation of the Word and a Christocentric interpretation of the world.

Christocentric discipleship challenges both students and teachers, whether in the academy or the church, to recognize Christ's lordship and significance in every realm of knowledge. Reformed thinkers, our fellow Christians of the past and present, spur us on to that end to help us see the applicability of Christocentrism to both God's Word and God's world. It is a beautiful portrait with layer upon layer of masterstrokes designed to reflect the light of God's glory and truth. As we ponder tough questions, we come to appreciate and take joy in the rational, biblical basis we have for the unity between truth and life. Christocentric teachers invite students to do the same, clearing as much as possible the obstacles that obscure their sight from looking to God alone for salvation. Ultimately, all Christians are learning to joyfully take up the tools of education, to paint their own lives' portraits, as it were, and live out different callings in the context of faith and allegiance to Christ alone. In doing so, it is the Holy Spirit who ultimately equips believers to produce an individualized Christocentric portrait of themselves. Christ in us, the hope of glory (Colossians 1:27).

As believers we gratefully and humbly carry out our callings, sometimes crying and sometimes laughing, sometimes half-heartedly and sometimes with caffeinated enthusiasm, sometimes falling short and sometimes being disappointed, and forgiving ourselves and others while seeking forgiveness from our King, knowing that if our great God is for us, who can be against us?

The Christocentric worldview, as Reformed thought envisions it, is the only framework that provides coherent answers to the profound questions of human existence. Secular education introduces questions to children at a very young age and is continually revisiting and addressing them inadequately—*No! Contrary to the Lord of truth!* A distinctly Christocentric education, whether at home, the church, or the academy, is the only context offering neither candy-coated despair nor candy-coated delusion. Christian teachers need to subjugate their own God-limiting education by drawing from the arsenal of rational scriptural considerations to promote God's kingdom through education to our students.

Many people will disagree with our efforts. Many will oppose our endeavors. But regardless of the opposition from without or our own inadequacies from within, the important thing is to have our God's approving eye upon our service for Him. Loving God with all our minds means we recognize that His lordship over all things, visible and invisible, is the most satisfying thing for Christian teachers and learners. For in so doing, we are satisfied by God Himself while savoring His grace in granting us the privilege to enjoy fellowship with Him. Through a due use of the ordinary means of learning, we can glorify Him in the enjoyment of unity in all truth for all of life.

Christ's scope and scepter extends throughout His Word and His world. Christocentric readers and teachers of the Bible have the unique opportunity to give others a radiant glimpse of Christ in all of Scripture for all of life.

Who else can say that?

Appendix

We Distinguish?
Biblicism, Boogeymen, and Bereans

Introduction

Disputes among Christians on social media are funny—until they aren't. When things heat up, it's either someone's intelligence, integrity, or their orthodoxy being questioned. When things cool down, we are told to keep discussions focused on doctrines, not dudes. But a partisan spirit is difficult to avoid. It even invaded the early church when various factions in Corinth claimed, "I am of Paul," "I am of Apollos," "I am of Cephas," "I am of Christ." The same thing can be seen in discussions of the needlessly frustrating topic of biblicism.

The topic of biblicism has flared up in recent years and shows no signs of riding off peacefully into the sunset. I have for the most part avoided participating in such debates and discussions online because they have been addressed by various authors, pastors, and laypeople ad nauseam. We are at the point where blogs, videos, and podcasts are frequently referencing biblicism as a foil to confessionalism and occasionally getting both wrong. Ironically, more heat than light is spent on biblicism by anti-biblicists, and discussing it is not always profitable. What is biblicism and why does it matter?

According to the Merriam-Webster Dictionary, *biblicism* denotes "adherence to the letter of the Bible," and its first known use was in 1805.[43] However, no citation was given for this use. From this basic definition, no positive or negative connotation can be obviously or fairly derived. In contrast, many evangelical biblical scholars and theologians further define biblicism to have definite negative connotations, if not denotations.

One example is Michael F. Bird, who defines and describes biblicism in the following way:

> Biblicism is an approach that regards the Bible as the exclusive source for formulating Christian belief and practice with explicit rejection of the need for historical background, garnering wisdom from wider tradition, recognizing the influence of one's cultural location, and attaining insights from out-group perspectives *even as* it unconsciously replaces historical background with revered historical figures, rehearses its own tradition,

---

[43] *Merriam-Webster*, s.v. "Biblicism," accessed February 5, 2024, https://www.merriam-webster.com/dictionary/biblicism.

reifies certain cultural values, and reinforces in-group boundaries.⁴⁴

Another example is *The Heidelblog*, which notes,

> Biblicism is not the attempt to be faithful to Scripture (i.e., to be biblical). Rather, in its extreme form, biblicism is the attempt to read Scripture in isolation. It is the attempt to read Scripture in isolation from the rest of Scripture and in isolation from the ecumenical creeds and the confessions produced by the various churches. It is the attempt to interpret Scripture as if no one has ever read it before. It attempts to interpret Scripture in isolation from the history of the church and especially the history of interpretation. It is the attempt to interpret Scripture in isolation from systematic theology or apart from one or more of the other departments of theology (e.g., practical theology).⁴⁵

If these negative definitions are the gold standard, those believers who are self-consciously confessional (adhering to detailed statements of major biblical doctrines summarized in a system, such as the 39 Articles, the Westminster Confession of Faith, or the Second London Baptist Confession of Faith) in their faith cannot coherently be biblicists. After all, confessional Christians heartily embrace the wisdom

---

44   Michael F. Bird, "What Is Biblicism," *Euangelion* (blog), August 14, 2020, http://www.patheos.com/blogs/euangelion/2020/08/what-is-biblicism/.
45   R. Scott Clark, "Resources on Biblicism," The Heidelblog, https://heidelblog.net/biblicism/.

and deliverances of those who came before, the great cloud of interpretive witnesses whose shoes we are unworthy to unloose. Before the confessional Calvinist is satisfied, however, it would be fruitful to put the negative and pejorative meaning of biblicism to the test. After all, if there is acknowledgment of biblicism in the extreme form, might it be possible for biblicism to exist in a non-extreme or a non-pejorative form?

Digging a Little Deeper

Whatever one's perspective is on how Protestants, evangelicals, or confessional Calvinists should define and describe biblicism, an approach that favors assertion more than argument, pejoratives more than premises seems less than fruitful. This may be extremely difficult for some due to the axiomatic function biblicism plays as nothing but pejorative.[46] The bottom line is that biblicism is the boogeyman.

In his recently released book, *The Reformation as Renewal*, Dr. Matthew Barrett diagnosed biblicism by a cluster of "symptoms" and noted the term's presumed first use as a pejorative in 1827[47] without noting this employment was by a Roman Catholic priest.[48] Ironically, Barrett followed the priest's lead in employing a malady metaphor in that the priest described biblicism as a sickness "caught" and

---

46   One representative example of the claim that biblicism has always been a pejorative term describing an idea and practice that should be rejected is found here: "Biblicism w/ Pastor Steve Meister," August 3, 2023, video, http://youtube.com/watch?v=P5eLPBc-MbE&t=2289s.

47   Matthew Barrett, *The Reformation As Renewal: Retrieving the One, Holy, Catholic, and Apostolic Church* (Grand Rapids, MI: Zondervan Academic, 2023), 21.

48   Chris Whisonant, "On the Origin of the Term 'Biblicism,'" *Alpha & Omega Ministries* (blog), November 25, 2023, https://www.aomin.org/aoblog/reformed-baptist-issues/on-the-origin-of-the-term-biblicism/.

"spread." This omission of the author's identity as a Roman Catholic priest is vitally important due to the common Roman Catholic apologetic against *sola scriptura*, which was from that point on pejoratively labeled as "biblicism."[49] But it must be remembered that for the Roman Catholic Church, the canonical Scriptures alone do not rise to the level of being the Word of God unless correlated or conjoined with Tradition such that the Protestant position is inconceivable from the start. We must distinguish.

Does first derogatory or pejorative use of a term, however, determine its future use for all people and for all time? After all, the term *Christian* was originally used by infidels to label believers and persecute them on the basis of wanting to imitate Christ. "Look at them – they are little Christs." Early Christians, thankfully, had the holy moxie to embrace the term *Christian* as a badge of honor. And believers of all stripes, biblicist and confessionalist alike, have been known as Christians for two millennia. What infidels meant for evil, simple believers meant for good. This strategy of taking a pejorative label and embracing it has been repeated throughout Christian history. Consider the following terms for people all meant to injure but all embraced by their adherents for various reasons:

- Lutheran
- Calvinist
- Protestant
- Puritan

---

[49] Latest and most relevant research into the origins and early use of the term "biblicism" have further uncovered information that does not refute my thesis, but supports the necessity to properly distinguish it and not automatically reduce it to a pejorative term. Whisonaut summarizes:

What if some sincere believers, knowing biblicism's pejorative use in Romanist apologetics against s*ola scriptura*, want to embrace the label? If it is inherently naive or worse, it must be shown to be so. To the chagrin of some academically oriented believers and their enthusiastic acolytes (mainly online), these confessional biblicists consider it intellectually and devotionally virtuous. The absolute madmen!

Apparently, there may be versions of biblicism that are perfectly biblical and confessional, similarly to how there are versions of, let's say, free will and determinism that are biblical and confessional despite protestations to the contrary. After all, there are versions of "tradition" quite consistent with classical Protestantism, are there not? Rome may own the copyright on capital-T *Tradition* but not lowercase-t *tradition*. What if some sincere believers, whether learned or unlearned, embrace the label *biblicist* as an intuitive and natural outflow of faith in the precious promises of God found in the Bible?

Isaiah 66:2 says, "But on this one will I look on him who is poor and of contrite spirit, and who trembles at my word." This trembling at God's word is, as Matthew Henry comments, "an habitual awe of God's majesty and purity, and an habitual dread of His justice and wrath. Such a heart is a living temple for God. He dwells there, and it is the place of His rest. It is like heaven

---

"There are seven uses of the term from the 19th Century which we have detailed (I also noted some other 19th Century Catholics using it derisively, but which do not have any bearing except in seeing that the Catholics continued, after Finnigan, to use the term as synonymous with *sola scriptura*). Five of them are positive uses and two of them are negative. It should be noted that *only the two negative uses were mentioned by Matthew Barrett*. This would have the effect of leaving his readers with a skewed understanding of the earliest uses of the term in English."

and earth, His throne and His footstool."[50] So then, trembling at God's Word is tantamount to trembling at God Himself.

What would drive anyone pastorally, logically, biblically, to discourage someone from this type of biblicism? Certain pastors with specific sensibilities are happy to go beyond the previously mentioned malady metaphors concerning biblicism and go straight for the jugular and equate biblicism with an "idolatry of the letter" of Scripture.[51] What can that possibly mean when our Lord Jesus Himself says the "words that I spoke to you are Spirit and they are life" (John 6:63)? The literal is the spiritual and vice versa when it comes to the Bible. Do theological teachers give due respect to our Lord's elevation of the Word of God? I fear for the ones who do not.

The devil, however, is in the details of how to apply this in discussions of biblicism versus confessionalism. Who is most biblical, the non-confessional biblicist, the non-biblicist confessionalist, or the confessional biblicist? I know. Heads are exploding right now. But we must distinguish, right? Easier said than done.

DEFINING AND REFUTING BIBLICISM?

Recent opponents of biblicism have had varying degrees of success in offering definitions of what they oppose, in

---

Chris Whisonant, "Further Thoughts on the Origin of the Term 'Biblicism,'" *Alpha & Omega Ministries* (blog), June 17, 2024, https://www.aomin.org/aoblog/further-thoughts-on-the-origins-of-the-term-biblicism/.

50 "Isaiah 66," *Matthew Henry Commentary on the Whole Bible (Complete)*, Bible Study Tools, https://www.biblestudytools.com/commentaries/matthew-henry-complete/isaiah/66.html.

51 Echoing a 19th century Protestant source, Josh Sommer, "Sola Scriptura & Biblicism: What's the Difference," *Baptist Broadcast* (blog), February 20, 2023, https://thebaptistbroadcast.com//sola-scriptura-biblicism-whats-the-difference#.

large part, because they get its aforementioned true origins confused. Let me just mention a few. Davenant Institute produced a video titled "Is Biblicism Bad?" in which Alistair Roberts defined biblicism as "that elevation of the Bible to such a high level that it occludes other things that we need to take into account."[52] However, it must be noted that Dr. Roberts prefaced his definition with a recognition of the Bebbington Quadrilateral, in which biblicism is simply one of the four distinctive traits of evangelicalism denoting how they express their ultimate theological commitment.[53]

David Bebbington's fourfold classification of evangelicalism consists of conversionism, activism, crucicentrism, and biblicism in a non-pejorative, "phenomenological" sense.[54] So if biblicism is indeed irrefutably demonstrated to be theologically pejorative and sociologically good (or at least neutral), this prompts the question, Does that make evangelicalism into a wobbly Jenga tower seconds away from collapse? Maybe it does if we accept a pejorative sense of biblicism.

Back to Roberts's definition. Is it even possible to elevate the Bible to an unacceptably high degree and level? The divine and human author of Psalm 119, the longest chapter in the Bible about the Bible, might beg to differ. A more manageable portion of Scripture is found in Psalm 138:2. David remarkably raises the biblicist stakes and would seem

---

52   Brad Belschner and Alastair Roberts, "Is Biblicism Bad?", November 7, 2017, video, https://www.youtube.com/watch?v=LrTyM29XRNU.
53   Daniel C., "Evaluating the Bebbington Quadrilateral," *Daniel's Place: Reformata et Semper Reformanda* (blog), May 15, 2017, https://puritanreformed.blogspot.com/2017/05/evaluating-bebbington-quadrilateral.html.
54   Samuel Crossley, "Recent Developments in the Definition of Evangelicalism," *Foundations* 70 (Spring 2016): 112–33, https://www.affinity.org.uk/app/uploads/2022/08/affinity-foundations-70-spring-2016.pdf.

to ruin the cause of anti-biblicism, or at least of Roberts's definition of it. The psalmist and Holy Spirit state, "For you have magnified your word above all your name."

Christians are supposed to be the people of the book. Given God's own elevation of His Word, it would seem to eliminate the idea of it occluding anything worthwhile. All believers should be elevating the Bible to a maximally high degree. Our problems don't ever seem to be a supposed idolatry of the letter but a neglecting or supplanting of the letter.

Roberts attempts to make a curious point when he adduces the Bible's silence on an issue to illustrate the existence of an allegedly ethical lacuna of God's Word. Quite perplexingly, Roberts states that the Bible is silent on *necrophilia!* Is this simply an academic impulse to score points with anti-biblicist acolytes on a popular level? I do not think the probative task for anti-biblicism is served well with this type of evidence or argumentation.

Genesis 1–2 has something to say about sex, marriage, and fruitfulness. Moreover, the fullness of the meaning of marriage revealed in the New Testament has implications for the desecration of bodies that necrophilia involves. Robert's definition of biblicism did not specify in what sense the elevation of the Bible will necessarily lead to the occlusion of, let's say, natural law or ethical issues, such as the example of necrophilia. In fact, I find this whole approach to be a disingenuous downgrade, not worthy of serious discussion. In politics, if you're the first to mention Hitler, you lose. In Christian ethics, if you claim the Bible underdetermines whether necrophilia is licit, you lose. Necrophilia can quite reasonably be addressed biblically and confessionally as a sinful practice by a thoroughly Reformed exposition of the moral law of God. Anything outside the purview of licit sexual practices is sinful, whether it is explicitly found in Scripture or only implicitly. Anyone who thinks the Bible is silent on some moral issue ought to think about it more carefully.

Furthermore, biblical silence is not to be equated with not having an explicit verse directly addressing a particular issue. After all, even non-confessionalist Christians believe in the Trinity by good and necessary consequence ("necessarily contained" in Scripture, if you prefer as the Second London Baptist Confession states).

Speaking of good and necessary consequence (or necessarily contained), the Sadducees on one occasion argued similarly to Alistair Roberts in Matthew 22:23–33. They tried to score points against the Lord Jesus by posing a conundrum about the resurrection. They were under the false impression that Jesus was unsophisticated, ignorant, naive, and unbiblical.

Since the Sadducees judged that Moses was silent on the afterlife and a future resurrection of the body, they offered a *reductio ad absurdum*. They did so on the basis of their notion of special revelation's silence on the matter of the resurrection. Whose wife will a woman be at the resurrection if her previous seven husbands were brothers and all died successively? The Lord Jesus draws out two valid conclusions from supposed biblical silence. In doing so, He combats biblical superficiality rather than silence.

First, the purpose and function of marriage fulfill its design in this earthly life, and to assume marriage continues in the resurrection is wrong. Why assume that? Second, they failed to read Scripture correctly by failing to read it closely and canonically, since a central divine declaration would have established the truth of the resurrection: "I am the God of Abraham, the God of Isaac, and the God of Jacob." The Logos, Jesus, draws out the valid logical implication that God is not the God of the dead but of the living. It would seem that the necessity of the resurrection is required by the present tense *am* in God's declaration in relation to Abraham, Isaac, and Jacob. Leave it to Jesus to offer them a biblicist bone in their kebab. So much for idolatry of the letter.

Jordan Steffaniak of The London Lyceum provides another recent refutation of biblicism. Is he more successful than Davenant Institute's Alistair Roberts? Steffaniak describes biblicism as "a disordered love" with inevitably "corrosive" effects for both faith and practice.[55] Descriptions, however, are easier than definitions. In fact, Steffaniak confesses (pun intended) that there are, "several ways biblicism could be defined." This is the heart of the issue! As we have seen, biblicism has a consistent Roman Catholic pejorative definition motivated by an anti-Sola Scriptura apologetic interest. But Protestant use in the 19th century evolved from neutral, positive, and then pejorative (quite possibly due to the increasing abandonment of confessionalism and the increase of non-confessional traditions).

Biblicism nowadays does not enjoy a standard definition as other terms, like *infralapsarian* or *supralapsarian*, for

---

55 Jordan L. Steffaniak, "Everything in Nature Speaks of God: Understanding Sola Scriptura Aright," *Modern Reformation* 31, no. 3 (May/June 2022): 37, https://issuu.com/modernreformation/docs/sola-345_2022_05_mr_final2_singles.

example, do. And while the *infra* and the *supra* attached to the *lapsarian* objectively mean something, the same courtesy isn't afforded to *biblicism*. *Bibl* is sitting right there at the beginning of the word! Why greet it with crossed arms?

Steffaniak offers the following definition: "Scripture is authoritative for all concepts of God (and any other theological locus such as morality, anthropology, etc.) Therefore, theological commitments must emerge from Scripture alone and be consistent with Scripture. Intuition, creed, confession, tradition, or any other source is incompatible with the supremacy of the Scriptures."[56] He further adds that "such a hard version of biblicism as defined here is impossible," for it allows no extra biblical input for theological construction to faithfully maintain Scripture's supremacy and sufficiency.[57] So here the key distinguishing feature of biblicism contra genuine *sola scriptura* is the meaning and application of the qualifier *alone*. For our purposes, I will leave aside Steffaniak's representation of the role intuition, creed, confession, tradition, and such may play for a genuine *sola scriptura* view. The important point is that for Steffaniak, biblicism excludes those extrabiblical things as even subordinate authorities under Scripture as the supreme authority.

In the process of painting one's opponent into a corner in a dispute, one must be sure to wear the proper footwear to avoid being stained with paint oneself. Otherwise, it can be something of a Pyrrhic victory. In other words, it is better not to claim more for an argument than is warranted.

---

56   Steffaniak., "Everything in Nature Speaks of God," 37.
57   Steffaniak, "Everything in Nature Speaks of God," 41.

Steffaniak asserts that an insurmountable problem with biblicism as he defines it is that since it "is unfeasible to derive any theological concept from Scripture without a secondary means apart from Scripture," then even theology itself "cannot be done." Steffaniak further spreads the proverbial paint as he pushes his biblicist opponent into the corner by asserting even "the basic reading of the text and forming an idea of it is itself external to Scripture. Therefore, no one can consistently adhere to biblicism, because biblicism itself is a theological concept derived rationally from Scripture, and is thus unacceptable as a theory on the grounds of its own premise. Moreover, such a vision of theology is inconsistent with Scripture's own vision."[58]

Nobody is infallible. Despite good intentions, we can't always employ and display "serious thinking for a serious church," as the London Lyceum's motto states. I believe Steffaniak's argument above is not as cogent or sound as he imagines, at least from the perspective of, let's say, a confessional biblicist.

Many critical observations can be made, but I want to focus on certain details. To the best of my ability, Steffaniak's argument can be distilled in this way:

Premise 1: Biblicism maintains it is always feasible to derive theological concepts from Scripture alone without secondary means such as reason, creeds, or even the act of reading itself to form ideas in contemplation of Scripture.

Premise 2: It is unfeasible to derive any theological concepts from Scripture alone without such secondary means,

---

58 Steffaniak, "Everything in Nature Speaks of God," 41.

including the act of reading, because these would be distinct from Scripture.

Conclusion: Therefore, since the idea of biblicism must be derived from reading Scripture, it is self referentially incoherent, and it cannot be feasibly maintained.

Premise 1 is a proposition combining what biblicism asserts with what biblicism entails and thus assumes what has to be proved. This is the fallacy of begging the question. He explains that the act of reading is a secondary means of knowing or acquiring knowledge that is itself not derived from Scripture. He states that "contemplative reasoning is an essential part of theology if we desire to do anything more than the literal repetition of the Scriptures into which biblicism would lock us."[59] The confessional biblicist would not grant this entailment but would simply maintain that reading, like reason itself, is simply how God ordained image-bearers to come in contact with divine special revelation in textual form.

God designed and caused the verbal and plenary inspiration of Scripture to fit it into our cognitive faculties like hands into gloves. In principle, the adequacy of human language has been wedded to our cognitive faculties sufficiently to the purpose God ordained it for. It is, therefore, not apparent, much less proven, that the act of reading is a mismatch for maintaining the feasibility of deriving theological concepts from Scripture alone.

Speaking of which, Premise 2 seems to double down on requiring so-called secondary means beyond Scripture for theologizing. We need only to provide one example or instance of deriving a theological concept from Scripture alone without

---

59 Steffaniak, "Everything in Nature Speaks of God," 41.

a secondary means even if such theologizing is attributed to the simple act of reading. Where should the confessional biblicist look? To ask that is to answer it!

The answer to Steffaniak's hypothetical biblicism is found in offering counterexamples from Scripture, including (but not limited to) how the Scriptures witness to how the apostles and the Lord Jesus theologized. The problem is that Premise 2 seems to be formulated from a supposed self-evident truth. If I were ever to encounter a biblicist according to Steffaniak's definition, I wouldn't make Steffaniak's assertion of Premise 2. Instead, I will offer a markedly Protestant, evangelical, confessional, and, dare I say, biblicist answer.

Romans 4:3 says, "For what does the Scripture say? Abraham believed God, and it was accounted to him for righteousness." Also, continuing to verses 6–7, "just as David also describes the blessedness of the man to whom God imputes righteousness apart from works: Blessed are those whose lawless deeds are forgiven." Romans 4, where Paul argues for justification by faith alone, results in refuting Steffaniak's premise 2 as far as confessional biblicism is concerned. Why? Because the apostle Paul derived the theological concept and conclusion of justification by faith alone from the Old Testament narrative in Genesis 15 and from the poem of Psalm 32.

Not only can this sort of theologizing be feasible, but we must also remember by whom it must be feasibly maintained. Paul's audience at the Church of Rome were not sophisticated or philosophically inclined. They were merchants, the poor, the humble, the illiterate, and perhaps even slaves. Not all the members could read Scripture themselves, but certainly all heard the Scriptures being read collectively and publicly preached in worship services on the Lord's Day. Don't forget: "Faith comes by hearing and hearing by the Word of God." Since we all can feasibly theologize from Scripture alone whether we identify as biblicist or not, it does little good to demarcate supposed biblicism by such a strict definition with little practical reflection in reality. Protestantism is famous for theologizing from Sola Scriptura when it comes to justification, right? And the perspicuity of Scripture, right? Steffaniak's Premise 2 postulates too much for the confessional biblicist. Theologizing for the confessional biblicist does not make Protestant Christianity self referentially incoherent.

Sensing that this initial definition of a hard version of biblicism is difficult to maintain by an imaginary biblicist boogeyman somewhere out there, Steffaniak offers a "more nuanced route to a biblicist framework."[60] This more nuanced definition of a softer biblicism rejects that theologizing must be done by appeal to only Scripture, but by means of Scripture first, then by other sources as secondary. He defines this nuanced, softer form of biblicism this way:

> Scripture is authoritative for all concepts of God (and any other theological locus such as morality, anthropology, etc.). Therefore, theological commitments must emerge from Scripture first and be consistent with Scripture. Intuition, creed, confession, tradition, or any other source

---

60 Steffaniak, "Everything in Nature Speaks of God," 42.

is incompatible with the supremacy of the Scriptures if they are understood temporally prior to Scripture.[61]

Alas, in the end, this definition of a softer form of biblicism emphasizing temporal priority can be refuted as well. In most believers' experience encountering Scripture, their theological commitments are born of necessity by the temporal priority of whatever Scripture they are exposed to. It may not be their principle, but simply their practice. Again, most believers are common people, not seminarians or philosophers. Steffaniak's second definition prompts the need to further distinguish between de jure biblicists and de facto biblicists. He concludes by quoting approvingly from Michael Allen and Scott Swain that biblicism is ultimately the "bastard child nursed at the breast of modern rationalism and individualism."[62] That escalated quickly. Ironically, in the very next article of the same issue as Steffaniak's negative assessment of biblicism, the interviewed describes biblicism as "the Protestant conviction of sola scriptura: that the Bible alone is the final authority for Christian faith and practice" and in agreement with David Bebbington that "biblicism was meant to emphasize that evangelicals are orthodox Christians."[63]

Reality seems to reflect that biblicism is made out to be a mountain instead of being recognized as the molehill that it

---

61 Steffaniak, "Everything in Nature Speaks of God," 41.
62 Steffaniak, "Everything in Nature Speaks of God," 44, quoting Michael Allen and Scott R. Swain, *Reformed Catholicity: The Promise of Retrieval for Theology and Biblical Interpretation* (Grand Rapids, MI: Baker Academic, 2015), 85.
63 Timothy Larsen, "Evangelical Biblicism Over the Years," interview by Blake Adams, *Modern Reformation* 31, no. 3 (May/June 2022), 46, https://issuu.com/modernreformation/docs/sola-345_2022_05_mr_final2_singles.

really is. Not only must mature believers be able to distinguish rightly between sound and unsound doctrines, but they also must distinguish between people's teachability levels. The principled biblicist who proudly states, "No creed but Christ!" can be easily corrected. If the new believer displays hard or soft biblicist sensibilities, he should not be looked on as insidious or seriously in error. Best pastoral practices would seem to require the more mature believer to treat them with respect as one would a first century new convert if you were transported back to that time. A simple believer with a Bible in hand, the Holy Spirit in his heart, and patient pastors and teachers can turn the world upside down. If that's all he has, he has everything. Yes, there is growth in the school of Christ.

"No creed but Christ!" may have been a slogan known to some from certain denominations of yesteryear, but nowadays I mainly hear it from certain academics and their acolytes who parrot prepackaged anti-biblicist talking points. And as mentioned, the talking points don't even get the origin or use of the term correct and its subsequent modifications. In other words, the biblicist goalposts keep moving.

Can you imagine the inadequacy of these talking points to the naive sincere biblicist needing instruction? If you know of any non-denominational, Holiness, Assembly of God, Free Church, or run-of-the-mill Baptist biblicist, wouldn't reasoning and reading Scripture be more God-honoring and fruitful? The sincere believer may be anti-confessional with "biblicist" tendencies. He hears talking points that descend into ad hominem and wonders why it's a slam-dunk refutation of biblicism. Don't confessionalists, they may wonder, know about Paul and the Bereans?

It's as though some Reformed and Reformed Baptists (my own tradition) don't remember being pop-Arminians themselves and coming to accept the doctrines of grace (the so-called five points of Calvinism) through much struggle. Unfortunately, there are too many professing confessionalists who can't be bothered to respect the misguided believer operating under unbiblical assumptions, such as holding onto only explicit statements in Scripture.

A recent strategy among environmental activists is to claim "climate homicide." They are charging oil companies for culpability in causing extreme weather events, rising sea levels, and so on. But this charge is based on so-called "attribution science," which posits non-debatable connections between certain human actions and certain environmental effects. At this point, some Reformed Baptists are unwittingly adopting this approach, a sort of attribution theology saying biblicism leads to Rome.[64] Oh, irony of ironies! Soffei Finngan wished that were true. I fear this is nothing more than an empty attempt to virtue-signal one's own superior theology. It is more non sequitur than virtuous.

Conclusion

If at this point, dear reader, you are not closer to a standard technical definition of biblicism, agreed upon by all parties, it means that the parties involved are talking past each other. Biblicism is an equivocal boogeyman—but a boogeyman nonetheless. That is why I prefer *Berean*. It's biblical and fits quite comfortably with my confessional Calvinism. During

---

64 "Biblicism w/ Pastor Steve Meister."

one of the apostle Paul's missionary trips to Europe, he preached before a group of northern Greeks. They were in all probability Gentile converts to Judaism known as God-fearers. They attended a local synagogue when Paul visited, as was his custom when he traveled to preach the gospel. Paul would preach Jesus from the Old Testament Scriptures, and instead of closing their minds to Paul's message, they exercised a nobility or fair-mindedness to search the Scriptures daily for themselves. Why? To find out whether the things Paul preached were so. Paul reasoned with them from the Scriptures with a view to persuading them of the person and work of Jesus. The Bereans "received the word with all readiness" (Acts 17:11). Test the spirits!

We started by offering some current definitions and descriptions of *biblicism*. We learned that it was commonly, though not originally, used as a Romanist approach to deride Protestantism's formal principle. Though commonly cited without revealing his identity and status as a Roman Catholic priest, *biblicism* as such, can only be pejorative since it is simply the equivalent term to the Protestant *sola scriptura*.

But it never seems to dawn on many current confessional Protestants zealously advocating for the pejorative use of *biblicism* that the term was originally neutral or positive. Subsequent common use had to change from a neutral or positive definition to a pejorative for its apologetic Roman Catholic employment against Sola Scriptura.[65] If Roman Catholic apologists, authors, and priests of the past enjoy the privilege of redefining terms in their favor and for their

---

65 See note 47 and 48 above.

use, why can't anyone else? Horror of horrors, what if some confessional calvinists want to retrieve the term *Biblicism*? Seems that chronological snobbery is a two-way street. After all, abuse of a term does not nullify proper use. Confessional Biblicists are quite comfortable with other terms and concepts such as Rule of Faith, catholicism, and catholicity to name a few. Biblicism would be no different. We must distinguish correctly.

Confessional Calvinists with thick skin like me yawn at being labeled "hyper-Calvinists" by people in other Protestant or evangelical traditions. Adding one more pejorative like *biblicist* doesn't faze me. It's mind over matter: if I don't mind, it doesn't matter.

Next, we gave a Davenant Institute definition. It wasn't the worst. It had the virtue of being polite, but then Davenant got deviant with the example of necrophilia. At least they acknowledge Bebbington's Quadrilateral, in which *biblicism* was used non-pejoratively.

With tongue firmly planted in cheek, I say Bebbington may not have ultimate authority on evangelical church history, but he has more authority than the Roman Catholic priest Finngan (apparent originator of the use of the term *biblicism* as the pejorative equivalent of *sola scriptura*). Then we discussed Jordan Steffaniak's definitions of hard and soft versions of biblicism. I think I showed that a biblicist worth his salt can effectively avoid being painted into a corner, and perhaps simultaneously showing that Steffaniak cannot avoid being splashed and stained by paint himself.

Last, we looked with only the briefest of a sidelong glance at a popular-level Reformed Baptist strategy that just baldly states that biblicism leads to Rome. But that's just attribution theology. It's also maximally ironic given Soffei Finngan's apparent origination of the pejorative use of the term as a Roman Catholic priest. Biblicism must be acquitted of committing some heinous crime. Confessional Biblicism can stand tall. It does not need to be quarantined as a contagious malady. Historically and theologically, he who distinguishes well teaches well.

Words are like bodies of water. They inspire or cause dread. Oceans can be tranquil or rage violently. Lakes can nourish or be polluted. Rivers can flow calmly or cause destruction. Biblicism displays the life of a river. I was taught that rivers originate from an elevated source. From there, gravity and the force of its forward movement gives it its shape, size, and depth. Because of those factors, over time, erosion causes the shape and direction to twist and wind. Eventually, rivers curve so much that they become oblong and almost touch. From that point, they eventually unite and become straight again. When defined derogatorily, Biblicism is like the Ganges River. When defined confessionally reflecting the Bible's own self attestation, Biblicism is like the River of Life: pure, clear, proceeding from the throne of God and of the Lamb (Revelation 22: 1). Biblically considered, may this treatment of the issue bring readers lasting benefit.

"Remind them of these things, charging them before the Lord not to strive about words to no profit, to the ruin of the hearers."

(2 Timothy 2:14)

www.ingramcontent.com/pod-product-compliance
Lightning Source LLC
Chambersburg PA
CBHW060322050426
42449CB00011B/2600